Kali in Bengali Lives

Kali in Bengali Lives

Narratives of Religious Experience

Suchitra Samanta

Foreword by
Susan McKinnon

LEXINGTON BOOKS
Lanham • Boulder • New York • London

Published by Lexington Books
An imprint of The Rowman & Littlefield Publishing Group, Inc.
4501 Forbes Boulevard, Suite 200, Lanham, Maryland 20706
www.rowman.com

86-90 Paul Street, London EC2A 4NE

Chapter 4 is a revised and expanded version of Samanta, Suchitra. 1998: "The Powers of the Guru: Sakti, "Mind," and Miracles in Narratives of Bengali Religious Experience" in Anthropology and Humanism, Vol. 23 (1):30-50.

Chapter 8 is a revised and expanded version of Samanta, Suchitra. 1994: "The 'Self-Animal' and Divine Digestion: Goat Sacrifice to the Goddess Kali in Bengal," in *Journal of Asian Studies*, Vol. 53 (3):779-803.

British Library Cataloguing in Publication Information Available

Library of Congress Cataloging-in-Publication Data Available

ISBN 978-1-7936-4633-0 (cloth)
ISBN 978-1-7936-4635-4 (pbk)
ISBN 978-1-7936-4634-7 (electronic)

This book is dedicated to my father, Dr. Sushil Kumar Bardhan Ray (March 1, 1918–April 22, 2009), and with joy. The Bengali word ananda, *suggesting an emotion beyond mere happiness, is more appropriate here, because I have been able to finally complete this book, whose research was conducted while I spent precious months with him in Kolkata. My father provided me the means to start afresh at the University of Virginia after a divorce. It would be much later that I could reflect on the courage it had taken for him to raise two young daughters after my mother's early demise, and to give up on a successful career in the Indian military's Medical Corps so that he could keep our young family together. Yet, he rose to be regarded in Kolkata, in a private capacity, as a highly-regarded radiologist. His long and lonely life inspired me to learn of discipline and forbearance in the face of obstacles, to persevere and to prevail, to live simply. He also shared with me, over the years, stories of rituals to the Sakti goddess at his paternal home in (now) Bangladesh. A framed picture of Kali's saint Ramakrishna hung on his bedroom wall, along with a photograph of my mother, Surabala (nee Karmakar), also a doctor whom he had met in medical school in British India (and on whose life I have published elsewhere, also in tribute). As my father grew older, more frail, and unable to go out himself, I brought back from my trips to various Kali temples in Kolkata the red hibiscus flower special to Kali, and garlands of marigolds for the portraits on his wall. The research for this work was facilitated by his reassuring presence, which has always been with me, even at a distance in the United States, and even after his passing. It is appropriate in so many ways that I dedicate this book to his memory, with love, respect, and gratitude.*

Contents

Foreword

Fierce, bloodied, and garlanded with severed heads, the sword-wielding Hindu goddess Kali is fearsome and awe-inspiring; yet for her devotees, she is also a deeply compassionate and loving Mother who offers salvation. Both Time as immanent and as transcendent, Kali is divinity as extreme paradox.

Anthropologist Suchitra Samanta is a superb guide to the complexities of the goddess Kali—offering us indigenous perspectives into the reality of the goddess as she is experienced in the lives of her urban, educated, Bengali worshippers. Drawing upon anthropological fieldwork in Kolkata, India, as well as her understanding of key Hindu religious concepts, Samanta provides a vivid account of the goddess Kali, of her devotees, and of the religious experiences and practices that powerfully transform their lives.

At the center of Samanta's account of Kali devotees are their ineffable experiences of the goddess, who becomes manifest to them in predictive dreams, bright and inexplicable lights, reincarnations, and the otherwise enigmatic actions of humans and animals. Samanta guides us deftly through an experiential landscape that is illuminated by devotees' understandings of the play of divine force and energy (*Sakti*), and the processes through which *Sakti* is revealed as knowledge (*sruti*), remembered in narrative (as *smrti*), and reflected upon in the workings of the mind (*man*). As she traverses this landscape, she takes us along both the "outer" and "inner" pathways to knowing Kali, as well as into the realms of sacrificial offerings (*balidan*) and of guru-disciple relationships.

Most importantly, Samanta listens attentively to the ways that devotees of Kali describe their experiences of the goddess and she provides us with their narratives—what she calls "spiritual autobiographies"—so that we can listen and learn, too, from their accounts. From these narratives we learn about the intense sensory experiences through which Kali reveals her presence in the lives of her worshippers. We learn about the many diverse ways that gurus—who are themselves conduits for Kali's *sakti*—intuit their disciples' needs and desires, and become healing, transformative forces in their lives. We learn that, although devotees' experiences of the divine are perceived to be "without logic," they nevertheless affirm the reality—and meaningful-ness—of Kali's divinity in the crises and complexity of their lives. We learn, finally, how the goal of religious self-discipline is ultimately to achieve a state of quiet and stillness, of oneness with Kali, beyond time and space and all worldly polarities. This *is* Kali's "meaning."

In *Kali in Bengali Lives* Suchitra Samanta has given us an eloquent and marvelously rich account of how religious experience—here of Kali the Mother—not only reveals the "meaning" of this paradoxical goddess in Bengali life, but also points to larger ontological truths about human existence. Reading *Kali in Bengali Lives* is, itself, a splendid journey of revelation.

Susan McKinnon
Professor of Anthropology
University of Virginia
March 2021

Preface

I explored various options for a dissertation topic in the graduate program at the Department of Anthropology, University of Virginia, including more feminist ones such as the status of women in India. I settled on my own observations of how the Hindu goddess Kali was perceived by Bengalis, especially as I had seen this in my own Bengali paternal family. I felt that I could perhaps offer another and "inner" perspective to this outwardly fearsome goddess in iconic representation, and as fierce demon-slayer in myth. I had heard stories of a family which had celebrated annual festivals in their home in now-Bangladesh (which they had had to leave just prior to Partition and Independence in 1947, for Kolkata), and a grandfather who had established a small temple to Kali, and had decreed that no animal sacrifices would be offered there. In other words, my impressions were of Kali as a protective and maternal presence. As I wrote a dissertation proposal I learned from the "father" of Kali studies in the West, David Kinsley, of Kali's long and complex history and changes to her meaning and significance over time. My intent was to complement, but also possibly offer other, specifically Bengali perspectives to existing studies.

I left for Kolkata in late summer of 1986 with both research agenda as well as a personal one, that of being with my aging father, long alone after my mother's early death. But the goddess, in keeping with her reputed unpredictability, entered my endeavors in ways I did not expect, and I came upon the accounts of religious experiences, as I see it in retrospect, serendipitously. I intended to begin my field research with standard anthropological methods, by observing Kali's devotees at temple and home and inquiring into the symbolic meaning of her rituals and their contexts. Very early on, however, I learned that my participants would give short shrift to such questions and turned the conversation around to what their Mother Kali "really meant" to them. Most would explicitly describe themselves as *bhakta*s, "devotees," with sometimes a family tradition of a special affiliation with Kali (but sometimes with other deities as well, like the god Krsna). As we conversed, they shared, in abundance, accounts of miraculous experiences associated with the goddess and her rites. I was initially at a loss as to what I should do with "data" that answered my initial research question but in a way I had not anticipated. Their perceptions of their Mother Kali—my central question— were expressed in narratives of personal experiences of the goddess in their everyday lives, such as precognitive dreams, mobile lights with no obvious source, inexplicable human manifestations where people were agents of divine will, and more. They asserted that there really was no logical *explanation* of such experiences, but interpreted those experiences, when I asked, or they sometimes volunteered, as the "play" of Sakti, the unpredictable workings of divine "power." They also discoursed on indigenous concepts of such "experience" itself, *anubhuti*, as intuitive glimpses into divine mystery. But, such experiences, they said, also suggested Kali's compassion, maternal love, and protection, her evident and manifest presence in the lives of her devotees. Kali *became* their mother in their experience of her *as* one. In their general impatience with my questions about ritual, implicitly but sometimes explicitly, my participants told me that their experiences of Kali took priority over exegetical discourse or analysis, and that a different kind of "knowing" was involved. In other words, her "meaning" in text and ritual became through personal experience of her, meaningful and real. Such events, as I recount their words and stories through this book, affirmed their efforts to know what Kali *truly* meant, how such experiences impelled them on the road to faith, confirmed that faith over time, and ultimately, transformed them, suggesting their *actual* identity, beyond the bounded reality in which we live in the world. So, asked some, who really am "I"? They were powerfully moved by their experiences, and they felt that I would believe them, as a fellow Bengali who shared an ethos with them, and respect what they had to say.

My participants also warned me that my "path" to learn about Kali would be a difficult one. She would not, they said, make it easy for me. They were right. The periods of field research and writing over the years would be rocked by turbulence in my personal life, prolonged ill health, and financial hardship. However, this "path," some said, was a journey that had begun earlier, and spanned many lives. Such an "identity," in their view, explained my presence in the here and now, and my particular inquiry, and thus, it was imperative that they respond. It gives me pause that my own journey—as I know it—has, again serendipitously, brought me to this book late in the day when I had long changed research interests to feminist inquiries on gender, minority status, and education, in India and in the United States!

Perhaps the journey to this book began many lives ago, as my participants suggested. But we have no answers, we cannot, they often reflected, when sharing their own stories. Indeed, neither do I, nor can I. For now, this is a book that gives voice to the miraculous experiences of "ordinary" people, not mystics or saints, and serves as "record," *smrti*, of the Bengali experience of their Kali.

Acknowledgments

My gratitude is due to so many: to Alokebabu, priest of Kali (whose real name I cannot reveal as he features so centrally in my book), who guided me to most of the people I write of; to Sri Rabindra Mohan Roy and his son Amlan Kanti Roy for their assistance in many ways and with so much affection (I am "older sister" indeed to Amlan); to my participants, devotees of Kali, who invited me to their homes, and who opened their hearts to me as they shared their experiences of the goddess in their lives.

My thanks are due to the members of my doctoral committee at the Department of Anthropology, University of Virginia, Professors Ravindra Khare (chair), Walter Hauser, H. L. Seneviratne, and Susan McKinnon, who read and helped me to improve my dissertation—from which kernel this book emerged decades later. In particular, I am especially and deeply grateful to Dr. McKinnon, whose compassionate support as mentor in every sense of the word sustained me through the often-difficult period of my years in graduate school, and who continues to advise and guide me today, and who wrote the foreword to this book.

At Virginia Tech my warm thanks are due to my colleagues, professors Barbara Ellen Smith and Katrina Powell for their professional but also moral support. I am especially grateful to Dr. Smith for her encouraging and enthusiastic response to the first, much shorter early draft of this book, and, over the years, for her friendship.

I warmly acknowledge my debt to my graduate teaching assistants, (now) Drs. Lipon Mondal and Inaash Islam for their help with the manuscript, in different capacities, at different stages. I would have found it hard to move forward without their assistance.

I am grateful to my family: my sister, Sumita Pillai, and my brother-in-law, Rear Admiral Sampath Pillai, for taking on the difficult task of caring for my father in their home in his last years, and seeing to his comfort and well-being with meticulous dedication, when I was too far away, and could not; and Pancha and Parul, poor themselves yet loyal, devoted attendants to my father—both are truly family.

I am grateful, simply, to have my courageous daughter Shahana, the good man, her husband David Joseph Hanley, and my two beautiful grandchildren, Haas Ravindra (10) and Sova Maya (6) in my life.

And last, but far from least, I acknowledge my two rescued Border Collies, Patches (February 1994–October 2008), and Gracie (December 2008–August 2020). Brilliant, funny, a TV addict, Patches made me laugh. She died on Kali's annual festival, and those who had met her, or knew of her, and unasked, said prayers on her behalf at Kalighat Temple, and at a church in Kolkata. Gracie arrived on New Year's Eve, a gift of sweetness itself, my boon companion and still center in the storms that beset my life in the years to follow. Both, in their high intelligence, protection, and devotion graced my life when I needed it most.

Introduction

She who is fierce of face;
Terrifying;
Whose unbound hair flies towards the South;
Who wears a garland of severed heads;
Who holds in her lower left hand a recently severed head,
In her upper left hand, the sword;
Making gestures of boon-giver and dispeller of fear
With her lower and upper right hands;
She whose tongue lolls;
She who is the color of clouds, and is dressed in space;
She whose body is drenched by a river of blood from her garland;
Adorned at her ears with two infant corpses;
She who has fearful protruding teeth;
Her breasts are large and uplifted;
She whose gaze is terrifying;
A belt made of the severed arms of corpses encircles her loins;
She is smiling;
Her mouth and lips are bloody,
Her voice is deep and loud;
Dweller in cremation grounds;
Her three eyes are as bright as the sun;
Beneath her, lies Siva as a corpse;
In all four directions jackals make a terrifying sound;
With Mahakala [Siva], Kali is in coitus;
Her Lotus-face is happy and smiling;
If you meditate on her in this form, all prosperity will be yours.

—*Tantrasar* by Krishnanand Agambagish (1604)[1]

1

The meditation,[2] above, of the goddess as Daksina Kali, is attributed to an early seventeenth-century spiritual "adept," *sadhak*, Krishnananda Agambagis, and appears in his compilation of texts, the *Tantrasar*, published about 1604 CE. As my participants told the story to me, Agambagis dreamed that the deity demanded that she be given an iconic form. He awoke, but did not know what this form should take. When he looked outside his home, however, he saw a dark-skinned woman in the vicinity of his home. Taking this to be a sign, he described his vision of Kali, which begins this Introduction, to meditate upon.[3]

Kali is regarded today as a major deity in the pantheon of Hindu deities worshiped largely across the state of West Bengal and also by Bengali Hindus in the predominantly Muslim nation of Bangladesh. However, versions of Kali are also worshiped across India, in the states of Assam, Kashmir, Punjab, Himachal Pradesh, Kerala, and Tamil Nadu, which are diverse by ethnicity and language, as well as in other South Asian nations such as Sri Lanka and

Figure 0.1   Graphic of Kalighat Temple Kali, print purchased at Kalighat, Kolkata, 1987.

Nepal (McDermott & Kripal 2003, 4). She also has a presence in the Bengali diaspora (McDermott 1996).

There are several Kali temples in Kolkata, as well as in Bengal generally (Roy 1986). Kalighat Temple, however, is the main pilgrimage site for worshipers of Kali, and attracts thousands on especially auspicious occasions such as her annual festival (Kalipuja), in the seventh lunar month of Karttik (October–November).[4] This is the most sacred locale of Kali in India, and the site's origin myth draws from the myth of the goddess Sati, who, angered by her father's insult to her husband Siva, sacrificed herself in fire. As Siva, in his grief and rage, carried her body across the worlds and threatened their existence, the god Visnu, (who preserves the universe), sliced the corpse with his discus, strewing the parts on earth. These fell at fifty-one places across the Indian subcontinent, each today a sacred pilgrimage site for a particular Sakti[5] goddess. The four toes of Sati's right (*daksin*) foot fell at the site of present-day Kalighat Temple.

Variants of Kali's icon draw from a basic template of a dark or blue-black deity, "Syama," both her dark color and another name for Kali, in hymns.[6] The goddess is represented as wearing a garland of skulls, having two or more arms which wield weapons, and makes gestures of protection and salvation. Daksina Kali, the four-armed variant of the goddess' icon, is the patron deity of Kolkata and associated particularly with Kalighat Temple (See Figure 0.1). Worshipers range across gender, caste and class, and even creed, seeking *darsan*, or "auspicious viewing" of the four-foot high ovoid black stone, Kali in aniconic form, at the center of the Temple's sanctum. Four solid silver arms, donated by worshipers, adorn this version of the deity. The stone was discovered in brilliant and inexplicable light by a mystic meditating in the dark forests that have now been replaced by a modern city with a population of millions.[7] While Daksina Kali is also so-called because she is represented with her right foot on the god Siva beneath her, *daksin* also means "south," and Daksina Kali's image at the Temple and during ritual worship at her festival (in worshipers' homes) faces this direction, which is that of death (ruled by Yama, god of death), over which she offers dominion. The gods reside in the high Himalayas to the north.

During my two phases of research in Kolkata, doctoral (August 1986–March 1987), and postdoctoral (September–December 1992),[8] I observed rituals for Kali at participants' homes and at her annual festival, and spoke with priests, scholars, and participants. While I would meet some few participants by the snowball method, through other people, my participants were drawn primarily from men and women who visited a smaller Kali temple[9] on the banks of a narrow and turgid tributary of the Hooghly River, the Adi Ganga (the "original" Ganga), about a mile from Kalighat Temple, in southern Kolkata. I was given access to them, appropriately, by its priest, Aloke

Bhattacharya (who was addressed with respect as Alokebabu,[10] including by myself), who also officiated at the time as one of four chief priests at Kalighat Temple. My personal acquaintance (and that of my family's) with Alokebabu was a fortuitous one. He had served as priest at family weddings and funerals, including at my mother's funeral in 1965. A well-known and respected preceptor (guru) and reputed Tantric adept, Alokebabu would serve as guarantor for my personal and professional integrity and introduce me to those worshipers who came to his temple. I would then visit the homes of these people, sometimes more than once, after I had asked them for permission in person at Alokebabu's temple, or by phone. In a particular set of ethnographic circumstances and my research question, my interviews were necessarily semi-structured, involving my open-ended questions, participants' responses, and often simply conversations, which I mostly taped (or recorded in writing shortly after I had met a participant). Especially as a woman, in this cultural context, I could not approach strangers, I realized early on, without Alokebabu's guarantee. Hence, my participants were almost always selected for me by the priest, people he felt could best answer my questions, often with the observation, "He (or she) is a great devotee."

Over my two phases of fieldwork I spoke with about thirty-five individuals and their families, one-third of whom were women. I found considerable variety in the ritual expression of devotion as well as greater or lesser degrees of exegetical knowledge among my participants, who belonged largely to the Brahman and Kayastha castes. They were literate, mostly of middle- or lower-middle-class status, small businessmen, musicians, and clerical officials. I would also speak with a young surgeon, and a journalist who claimed royal antecedents, eight women, again ranging across the class spectrum, none but two working outside their homes. My interviews were conducted in Bengali. In sum, the voices I present in this book, in different contexts, are diverse by gender, caste, and class. Alokebabu, a Brahman himself, carried the authority of spiritual stature. The people he suggested I speak with were, in some cases, his disciples who saw him as their guru. Others were visitors to his temple, like the young surgeon. I myself did not design my research inquiry on the basis of gender, class or caste, but broadly on Bengali perceptions of Kali. However, as I would find, Alokebabu would be the person who directed my inquiry toward those he saw as devotees, and to whom I would have access.

My participants, Kali's devotees, were, I found, especially influenced by the Advaita school of philosophy (which holds divinity as "nondual"), and Bhakti devotionalism.[11] The books they read, and the views they cited came from the books and commentaries on the Upanisads (the Vedanta) available at the Ramakrishna Mission Institute. Most were familiar with the words of Ramakrishna (1836–1886), collected in the *Kathamrta*,[12] and anecdotes from the life of his disciple Vivekananda (1863–1902). Thus, themes from Vedantic commentaries on a unitary divinity, Brahman, and from devotional Bhakti beliefs, and its many divinities, were included in the exegeses and stories I would hear about how worshipers experienced Kali. However, caste and economic differences appeared not to be dominant factors in worshipers' perceptions of Kali, a point made by many, in keeping with Bhakti ideology that divinity is accessible to all, across wealth, caste, and gender. What they did share was their perception of themselves as devotees of the goddess, or, had come to be such. However, I offer a note of caution here—while many contemporary Indians deny that caste hierarchies continue to distinguish people by social and birth group, I found that such views did prevail. On the one hand, Sachin, whose story appears later, describes his Brahman guru deliberately eating from the same plate as his lower-caste disciples (like Sachin, a Kayastha), to illustrate his transcendence of caste distinctions. Ananda, a Brahman bhakta, deliberately eats with Muslims at his sister's wedding. I myself, of Kayastha caste, would confront such distinctions at a female Brahman participant's celebration of Kali's annual festival at her mother's home. Bimala, while inviting me to participate and observe the rituals at her maternal home on this occasion also warned me that her mother "maintained" such distinctions. I was not to touch the items of worship, which would be polluted if I did so. I complied, interested in observing the rituals, and not jeopardizing my inquiry, or my relationship with Bimala.

My own paternal family's affiliation with Kali served me to advantage, I would discover. Kali's worshipers assumed my shared awareness of her significance in Bengali lives, and that I had some knowledge of Bengali aesthetics and culture. My particular situation as a Bengali woman, the mother of a daughter (then ten years old, who had accompanied me to Kolkata on my first phase of research), and speaking with fellow Bengalis—in Bengali—about their Mother Kali would, I realized in retrospect, "explain" the "data" I would get, in an abundance of stories of their personal—and (broadly) miraculous—experiences of her. They also assumed, I realized, that I would respect their experiences of Kali, in all the wondrousness of these accounts, and not dismiss such accounts as untrue and inconsequential. This was a real possibility, coming as I did from America, that bastion of science and technology, and possibly skeptical about accounts of the "miraculous" which my participants shared with me, and often with deep feeling. The one time I asked a male participant if he saw a contradiction between scientifically established facts, and *alaukik ghatana* (miraculous or extra normal events),[13] he looked at me in some surprise, and briefly replied in the negative, without explanation or any further discussion.

I would also see this everyday presence of the alaukik in speaking with my father, a reputed radiologist in Kolkata, thus a man of science, and a sharp, practical and skeptical man. To illustrate the simultaneous ordinariness, as well as extraordinary quality of an alaukik experience, in this case precognitive dreams of Kali, he recounted the two times, both related to crises in his life, where she appeared to him. In an earlier dream several years ago, Kali, he said, appeared to him naked (as in many iconic representations of her). He would precipitously leave a remunerative position he had held for many years at a prestigious nursing home in Kolkata, after a falling-out with hospital administration. However, he would find another position very soon after. He interpreted her appearing to him as predicting both loss, but also gain, a Mother's compassionate resolution of a problem. The second time he "saw" Kali in a dream was just before I was to depart for the United States, this time she was "dressed," that is, adorned and clothed. He was concerned about where he would find the finances for my studies abroad. But, as he recounted the dream to me (when I returned to conduct research), he again interpreted his dream in retrospect to mean that the goddess would see to my well-being (and indeed, he had found adequate finances for my first semester at the University of Virginia, proving what the dream had predicted). Having shared his two dreams, he briskly and immediately sat down to breakfast with me and evidently considered the matter closed to further discussion. His experiences, recounted, needed no further explanation. A female participant, Sumona, in much more difficult financial circumstances, after recounting her stories to me, would ask rhetorically, "Why would I then say she [Ma Kali] is not there?"

Conversely, there was also on the devotees' part an awareness of the now-expanded world of the diasporic Indian. This not only allowed for lively conversations, over cups of tea, about my life in the United States, but also established a relationship that allowed for their sharing of often very private and personal accounts that moved them to powerful emotion, often to tears. Even as they asserted a relationship with their Mother Kali, one that was ineffable and "could not really be expressed in words," they told me, in abundance, about their experiences of her. They also shared accounts of remarkable experiences related to their preceptors or gurus, perceived as conduit of her divine power as Sakti.

It is necessary and important to note at the start that a culturally unique perception of me was directly pertinent to, and which, I reflected in retrospect, resulted in the accounts I would hear. Several participants commented on the whimsical ways of an unpredictable deity, bringing me, a Bengali, all the way from affluent America to research a topic so close to their hearts. (I did not tell them that I was an impecunious graduate student.) They explained my presence and research focus by suggesting that some ancestor and Kali devotee in my family was, through me, fulfilling some undertaking left incomplete in an earlier life. My research, then, was essentially a quest, inspired by Kali herself, the mysterious "play," *khela*, of divine power, Sakti, working across space and time. My presence was, to my participants, explicable within this worldview and my questions needed an appropriate response. So, they spoke to me as a fellow devotee (defined simply by the nature of my inquiries, and not by any pretense to religiosity on my part), instructing me by story of how their mother Kali was *meaningful* to them in their lives—beyond of her "meaning" in text and scripture. I, of course, had no way of either agreeing or disagreeing about my "place" in this larger scheme of things as they offered *their* explanation for my presence in their lives, and my particular inquiry. These are my reflections in my journal, during the second phase of my work:

> With women, it is assumed that I will understand, as a woman myself. This is how I understand the less defensive, more open recounting of the alaukik in women's conversations with me. . . . [Their] stories involve, as a rule, the reso- lution of crises related to a loved one. However, my (quite genuine) assertion that I do believe in the possibility of such events, though I can prove nothing (that is not the point), results in a remarkable opening up of the Bengali devo- tional psyche. It is quite wonderful! I feel as if I am on uncharted seas, with no knowledge of a destination, no known goal. It is hard to remain unconvinced in the face of devotees' assertions that my own journey must have been foretold eons ago; that my meetings with people at this time was foretold, that I am playing out the "fruits" of my past actions, *karmaphal*. As a middle-aged man observed, perhaps I was his daughter in some previous life, and that our respec- tive spiritual selves are now meeting. Well, who knows? But such thinking makes my work into a mission—which is quite exhilarating! (October 3, 1992)

My participants' stories, thus, emerged apparently in dialogue between fellow devotees. Alokebabu would comment on *yatris*, "travelers," human agents employed to some intent by an unknowable divine will. A female participant in her early forties, whom I met in my second phase of work, a teacher in a Kolkata school and active in the theater world of the city, who had no miraculous experiences to share with me, expressed her belief that I was such a yatri, whose presence was otherwise inexplicable. My inquiry, about their perceptions of Kali, a project inspired by my own devotion, bhakti, and the divine force or power, Sakti, had evidently impelled such work—in *their* understanding.

Diana Eck eloquently describes the concept of Sakti, by which she has been moved, as *jagrata*, "alive."[14] This is a term often used by worshipers in relationship to sanctuaries of the goddess, like Kalighat Temple. As people in their hundreds (and more, on festive occasions) come to such places to pour out their grief, their supplication, and their devotion "in the midst of life" (Eck 2003, 138), Sakti is a palpable presence. I would sit on a wooden

bench within the Temple walls, watching worshipers offering prayers, walking around the Temple precincts, and visiting, within those precincts, the
shrines of other deities like Manasa, the Serpent Goddess, and the dark god,
Krsna. I found myself amazed, and like Eck, deeply moved at the sense of a
presence, its power, and could not explain it. But I loved what I sensed, and
I was drawn to the Temple and the spirit that filled it, powerfully, even as
I would spend much of my time at Alokebabu's little temple. In this book I
present the remarkable experiences I would hear, in personal stories, of Kali
in Bengali lives, stories that speak of spiritual journeys, of transformations
big and small. As I learned from my participants, and reflected on what I
learned, the journey has also been my own.

In chapter 1 I present a brief history of Kali over her long presence in its
many permutations in the Indian tradition, drawing from the "father of Kali
studies," David Kinsley (1975a), and perspectives from more recent Western
scholarship on the goddess. At the conclusion of this chapter I present my
own argument, both complementing Kali studies to date and also drawing
from my own data, the narratives of miraculous experience. I propose that
these accounts offer another perspective on Kali as Mother, and the divine
"force," Sakti, she embodies. In the accounts Kali the compassionate mother
is experienced as both "real," *asal*, in her intervention in devotees' lives, but
also, as Sakti, in the extraordinariness and unpredictability of the experiences,
pointing to an ultimate and transcendent reality, as "truth," *satya*, and offering a unique insight into the human-divine relationship in Hindu belief.

Chapter 2 presents the status of "veridical" or unmediated knowledge
(what I am calling "miraculous") as "valid" in Indian philosophical traditions,
a centuries-old epistemology which evidently finds continuity into contemporary times. In colloquial terms my participants comment on cultural concepts also described and debated in philosophical thinking, of "mind" (*man*),
"memory" and "recollection" (*smrti*), and "intuitive insight," or "experience"
(*anubhuti*) to interpret their experiences of Kali. These concepts, framed by
the larger and inclusive perception of the divine as Sakti, offer an indigenous
paradigm which presents an inner and culturally unique understanding of a
complex and paradoxical divinity, Kali.

Chapter 3 discusses Western scholarship on the expression of human experience in narrative. Experience itself is discussed (e.g., the distinction between
"an" experience, and "experience"), and its integral relationship to remembering, the selectivity of memory, and the structured expression of experience
in autobiographical narrative. Not only are there different types of narrative
(shorter and anecdotal; longer and chronological), and as I present in Bani's
experiences (chapter 6), a structure which is free-associative, but that there
is no one kind of autobiographical account, even within a culture. The telling of such accounts is culturally specific, and also specific to the narrator's

audience. This chapter also presents and discusses recent commentary by Western scholars, from religious studies and anthropological perspectives, on acknowledging the validity of other ways of knowing, questioning established Western paradigms which have been reluctant to admit such "other" episte-mologies, and resistant to the interpretation, in this case, of paranormal and psychic phenomena. In this context I discuss an edited volume that focuses on perspectives brought to bear on the miraculous specifically in different contexts in South Asian religious traditions (Dempsey & Raj 2008).

The narratives I present in part II, in chapters 4 through 8, range from those which are shorter and anecdotal to longer, more chronologically structured ones, one which is free-associative, and one which has to be largely elicited by me (Alokebabu's story, chapter 5). Concepts of Sakti, the *man*,[15] "intuitive insight" (anubhuti), and remembrance (smrti) provide the paradigm within which these narratives may be interpreted, as my participants speak of how they experience their mother Kali.

Chapter 4[16] frames in scholarship, in scripture, and in my participants' views the persona of the preceptor or guru, expressly acknowledged as Kali/Sakti's conduit across these diverse discourses, a persona invested with powers beyond the ordinary. In different contexts in this chapter I present accounts of experiences related to initiation by a guru, to his healing powers, and to the possibility of his rebirth into a beloved disciple's family.

Chapter 5 goes more in depth into one guru's life and experiences, in this case Alokebabu, and how he is perceived by his disciples and visitors to his temple as a man of great powers, both a Tantric and a devotee, bhakta. However, where scripture, scholarly discourse, and my participants' observa-tions all note the immense spiritual discipline that results in such powers, by the same token these may not be disclosed at risk of arrogance or charges of chicanery. My participants share *their* experiences of Alokebabu's powers even as he holds back from sharing any with me. He, does, however, share his views on his mother Kali, and on devotion (bhakti), his break with his fam-ily to pursue his vocation as Kali's priest. It is only at the very end that—by implication and not directly—he suggests to me his (possible) powers.

Chapter 6 presents and discusses the longest account I would hear, from Bani, a middle-aged woman, as she recounts, in a remarkable free-associative "spiritual autobiography" her initial fear of Kali, but then, in a journey over time and space, her experiences of the many gurus in her life (including Alokebabu), in person, in dreams, in objects given to her, which ends in her "receiving Kali." She comes, in the story she recounts to me, to finally under-stand (or, more accurately, "realize") this divinity whom she had once feared.

Chapter 7 focuses on experiences related to ritual practice. I frame the chapter around the symbolic meanings of colors, objects, and actions related to the ritual worship of Kali/Sakti. I structure this chapter around

"outer" styles of worship (more overtly ritualistic), and "inner" prefer-
ences (meditation-based). These are terms my participants themselves used
to distinguish ritual practice, while also asserting that both are a matter
of personal choice and of the *man*. Both yield "insights," anubhuti, into
divine power. While ritual worship as "inner" and as "outer" may and
do overlap, this is not necessarily gender-segregated but a matter of the
devotee's personal choice, how he or she prefers to worship Kali. I would
find the best accounts of the former associated with women's experiences,
and the latter, with men. I present the experiences of five women, and
three men, including the story of one woman who turns to atheism after a
personal tragedy.

In chapter 8[17] I present narratives associated with experiences related to
sacrificial offering as "gift," *balidan*, as animal or vegetable—a penultimate and powerful ritual for Kali/Sakti. A body of philosophical exegesis
and prescription in scriptural texts comment on this central rite, which I
discuss in framing the narratives in this chapter. Where, in the earlier chapters in this book narratives of experience speak to the miraculous as unsolicited and revelatory and personally transformative in life, experiences
related to sacrifice take on a cosmic significance. A "successful" sacrifice
(where the animal is killed cleanly with one stroke of the sword) ensures
the continued "well-being," *mangal*, of the devotee and even his extended
family. An "unsuccessful" sacrifice risks sudden death—his own, or in his
family, with implications for lives to come, as "calamity," *amangal*. His
moral integrity, the quality of his *man* is what is central, as he, essentially,
offers his own "animal-self" *pasujiva*, in sacrifice. In this chapter, accounts
describe participants' experiences, and those of powerful gurus who offer
sacrifice on behalf of a disciple, "taking on" the moral failings of the latter
in an act of great love and risk to themselves.

I end with my reflections in the concluding chapter on what my participants' experiences, expressed in narratives in different contexts, offer
as answer to my question: how do Bengali devotees understand Kali?
What does "intuitive experience" itself, as anubhuti, and locus of both
experience and interpretation, the *man,* have to offer prior interpretations
of this complex deity? The "miracle" lies less perhaps in the event than
in its *interpretation*, of what is being communicated. In an indigenous
paradigm the Mother Kali is experienced simultaneously as "real" in the
circumstances and exigencies of life, and the resolution of real life crises,
or simply and actually "seen." But such experience, by definition, is also
"true," in what it intimates about a larger reality, here Kali/Sakti. In their
own words, and their own stories of *experiencing* her, my Bengali participants, devotees of Kali, offer their understanding of the mystery that is
divinity—in its unpredictability but also its compassion.

NOTES

1. Author's translation.

2. I have not used diacritical marks through the book, but do so in an Appendix, with select names of deities, concepts, and Bengali terms which appear throughout, to mark the sounds and letters of the Bengali (or Sanskrit) alphabet as these should be accurately presented.

3. Krishnananda Agambagis, *Tantrasar*, edited by M. Chattopadhyaya, translated by C. K. Tarkalanka from Sanskrit to Bengali (Kolkata, Nababharat Publishers, 1982), 387. Some minor variations of this meditation appear in the ritual manuals for Kali's worship today, the *Srisri Kalipuja Paddhatis*, (1981, 1985). In another version from the same text, describing the "Kali of the cremation grounds." *Smasana Kali*, the goddess's "eyes are pink, her hair disheveled, her body gaunt and fearful." The worshiper is instructed to conceive of her "in this way" and worship her, naked himself, at the cremation ground (Kinsley 1996, 77).

4. The current Temple dates to 1802, and was built by a wealthy Bengali family who acquired the sixteen miles of land on which it stands from Moghul rulers of India in the sixteenth century. Its centrality was of such significance that English women would visit the Temple, bearing gifts (on Kalighat, see Basu Roy 1993; Alok Ray 1980; N. R. Ray 1980; A. K. Ray 1982; Ward 1822). Deonne Moodie addresses the initiatives at modernizing the Temple by Bengali middle classes (2018).

5. I use the upper case when referring to Sakti, feminine divinity as force or energy, and the lower case for sakti, when referring to human capacity.

6. There are eight official Kali icons, including "Smasanakali," "Kali of the Cremation Ground" (Swami Nirmmalananda 1970). The four-armed "Adyama," "Mother of the Beginning," is the Kali at Adyapith temple, and "Tarama," "Compassionate Mother," is at Tarapith temple. Both temples and sites of pilgrimage are near Kolkata.

7. According to literary references to the site dating back to the eighth century CE (Bagchi 1980; Roy & Upadhyaya 1983; Roy 1986).

8. Both phases of field research were funded by grants from the Institute for Intercultural Studies. The writing of chapter 8 was funded by a one-year fellowship from the National Endowment for the Humanities (1993).

9. Throughout this book I will use lower case for Alokebabu's temple, and upper case for Kalighat Temple.

10. All names have been changed.

11. Bhakti, as a powerful and diverse trend, across sectarian difference under the rubric of Hindu belief holds that social differences can be transcended by the power of devotion for a chosen deity. I discuss this in greater length in chapter 1. I use the upper case for the movement and set of beliefs that constitute Bhakti, and the lower case when referring to personal expression of devotion.

12. The *Kathamrta*, a collection of Ramakrishna's sayings, edited by Mahendranath Gupta, was published in 1902, 1904, 1908, 1910, and 1932. A listed publisher is Kathamrta Bhavan.

13. I use the Bengali word *alaukik* for a range of experiences, including waking visions, dreams, chance meetings, distance healings, and more, in reference to "extra normal" or "miraculous."

14. "Beyond body consciousness" were the words used by now-late Sri Rabindra Mohan Roy to explain this concept to me. I use Roy's real name as he was not a participant but a retired chemist and scholar who assisted me with the meanings of some concepts.

15. *Man* is a cognate of the English "mind" and derives from the Sanskrit *manas*. The faculty, and concept however, in the Indian (and Bengali) context means also a locus for emotion, and best translates as "heart/mind." I will use the word *man*, in italics, in this book.

16. This chapter is a radically revised and expanded version of Samanta, Suchitra. 1998: "The Powers of the Guru: Sakti, 'Mind', and Miracles in Narratives of Bengali Religious Experience" in *Anthropology and Humanism*, Vol. 23 (1):30–50.

17. This chapter is a radically revised and expanded version of Samanta, Suchitra. 1994: "The 'Self-Animal' and Divine Digestion: Goat Sacrifice to the Goddess Kali in Bengal," in *Journal of Asian Studies*, Vol. 53 (3):779–803.

Part I

FRAMING RELIGIOUS EXPERIENCE IN THEORY AND INDIGENOUS BELIEF

Chapter 1

Interpreting Kali

A History and Western Perspectives

KALI'S HISTORY

In this chapter I offer a brief history of a complex goddess and the changes in both her iconic representation as well as her meanings in Hindu belief and practice over a long period of time. I also offer, in brief, particular interpretive perspectives by Western scholars, and conclude this chapter by engaging particularly one such insightful interpretation by the "father of Kali studies," David Kinsley, as this informs my own. While he approaches Kali's meaning from a phenomenological perspective, and her role in text and myth over time, this book is also about what she means, but to her contemporary devotees—in their own words and stories, and how they experience her in their lives.

A goddess with a "multilayered history," Kali spans the range between demon-slayer, protector from disease, and loving Mother (Kinsley 1975a; McDermott & Kripal 2003, 4). With origins in pre-Vedic, pre-Aryan India (prior to 1500 BCE), this possibly once-tribal goddess entered the Sanksritic, Brahmanical textual tradition between the fifth and sixth centuries CE, in the *Devi-Mahatmya* (in the *Markendeya Purana*), as slayer of demons. In this text she emerges from the archetypical goddess Durga's anger-darkened forehead to destroy the prideful demons who threaten the hegemony of the gods and the moral order of the universe. Gaunt, with gaping mouth and lolling tongue, armed with sword and noose, Kali roars in rage and proceeds to decapitate two demon chiefs, Chanda and Munda. She appears again in this text to swallow the offspring of the ostensibly invincible demon, Raktabija ("drops of blood," each of which produces another demon), and then sucks out the blood from the demon himself (Jagadisvarananda, *Devi-Mahatmya* 8.40–63).

15

Between the eighth and sixteenth-century Kali comes into her own (as an "ontological absolute")[1] as Sakti, "energy or power," and as Creatrix, the chief deity of Sakta Tantrism, a body of beliefs and practices which took particular hold in the eastern and north-eastern regions of the sub-continent (present Bengal, Assam, and Nepal). The concept of Sakti emerges from the gender-neutral Brahman of the *Upanisads*, but as female, and like the Brahman is also, in conceptual continuity, the totality of cosmic manifestation (Foulston & Abbott 2009, 10).[2] Hence, in a Sakta text, the *Mahanirvana Tantra*, the male gods Brahma, Siva, and Visnu arise from Sakti, leaving her unchanged, like the earlier Brahman (Kinsley 1975a, 110).[3] Sakta philosophy holds that divinity is nondual, symbolically expressed in the complementarity of female and male, Kali and the god Siva, an origin myth which depicts goddess and the god in coitus. In this myth creation occurs when Subject (Kali) becomes aware of Object (Siva), and the world is created in the rhythms of Kali's dance: as male, female, light, darkness, space, time, life, and death. Kali-Siva is thus the beginning, the middle, and the end of creation. It is toward the bliss and stasis of that original conjoining and totality that the Tantric adept aspires to return.[4] By the seventeenth century, Kali is the loving albeit fierce and protective mother in the devotional discourse of Bhakti belief (McDermott & Kripal, op.cit., 4), and it is on her lap that the devotee, her "child," seeks shelter—a metaphor for the original state of nonduality and unity sought by the Tantric adept.

The Sakta saints Ramprasad Sen (1718–1775), Kamalakanta Bhattacharya (1769–1821), and Ramakrishna Paramahamsa (1836–1886) conceptually combined the Tantric Creatrix with the deity as Mother in the Bhakti (devotional) tradition, which arose in southern India about the seventh century CE, "touched" the Bengali worship of the god Krsna in the fifteenth century, and by the eighteenth century expressed itself in relation to Kali, adding the dimensions of compassionate, protective, and benevolent mother to her loving "child"—though with some tension between these trends (McDermott 2001, 3).

Bhakti expresses personal religious experience in poetry, prayer, and song, and emphasizes emotion in the human-divine relationship. Such access to the deity, ideally, knows no social boundaries of gender and caste, defined as it is by love, whole-heartedly offered by the human, and reciprocated by the deity, albeit in a hierarchical relationship, here that of mother and child. As concept and religious trend, Bhakti is "one of the most influential perspectives in Hinduism" (Prentiss 1999, 41). It is premised on the fact that the human heart is capable of love, a love, however, which may take different forms, depending on the deity involved (so a servant to a master, like the monkey god Hanuman in relation to Rama), or that between lovers (the god Krsna and his consort Radha). This trend under the rubric of Hindu belief is diverse, by social group, region, language, and specific Bhakti saints. McDermott, speaking of the diversity and inclusivity of Bhakti, calls it the "democratization" of love (2001, 6).

To my participants Kali is the normative and beautiful Mother despite her fearsome appearance, who evokes powerful emotions of both love and fear. She is stern yet accessible, the ultimate refuge in both a soteriological sense, but also in the exigencies of life.[5] My participants addressed, or referred to her always as their mother, Ma Kali, as did I in speaking of her with them. As the narratives of experiences in this book reveal, the compassionate (yet unpredictable) Mother Kali in devotional discourse, and the uncontainable and unpredictable "force" that is Sakti are conflated in participants' interpretations of miraculous events in their lives—as precognitive dreams, lights without obvious source, waking visions, as related to their gurus, the remarkable resolution of life crises, and more. Bani, a female participant whose experiences I present in chapter 6, replied, when I asked her how, given her earlier fears of Kali, she was drawn to the goddess, replied cryptically, by fear. When there is fear, she elaborated, there is bhakti. I would understand her to mean that Kali, a demon-killer and punishing deity in myth and icon, was difficult to comprehend, and for whom to feel devotion. Coming to love this complex deity required effort, on the difficult journey to faith.

WESTERN PERSPECTIVES ON KALI

Perceptions of Kali in the West have generally not been "overly favorable" (McDermott & Kripal 2003, 5), even as she has attracted considerable interest. These perspectives range from phenomenological studies of the goddess in text and myth, to the historical, the psychoanalytical, and feminist, offering interpretations of a complex, paradoxical, and evidently fascinating image of the divine in Hindu belief. McDermott and Kripal begin their book (2003) with an excerpt from a hymn by the eighteenth-century Kali devotee, Kamalakanta Bhattacharya:

I cannot fathom Her.
My whole life has passed
trying. [excerpt, n.p.]

McDermott and Kripal comment that Western scholars celebrate the goddess' "excesses of . . . power, sexuality, and violence, and the hidden potential of these energies to transform and liberate those who dare approach her" (9). The focus has been on her sexuality, social rage, as the slayer of demons in battle—in ways not familiar to Kali's South Asian devotees. Kali's multivalence and her transformative power as Sakti has, say these authors, allowed for the goddess to be seen beyond the specificities of South Asian geography and culture and made into an "ahistorical, archetypal feminist figure" (McDermott & Kripal 2003, 5). However, interest in Kali has been a sustained one over time. In colonial India Kalighat finds mention in the diaries and travelogues of British civil servants, and in the writings of missionaries, who comment on the barbarism and idolatry of non-Christian religiosity (as evident in the erotic acts and symbols of Tantric practices). Kali's association with the Thugs, bandits who strangled travelers, and then offered their victims as sacrificial gifts to the goddess, impelled military action by British forces in the 1830s. However, there were also scholars of Tantric texts, like Sir John Woodroffe (1865–1936), writing in the early twentieth century, who "explained" and defended Kali. Into the 1960s and 1970s, Western counterculture groups turned to India, Hinduism, and Tantra, seeking meaning outside the Judeo-Christian tradition, and "apologetic" works such as by Rawson (1973), and Mookerjee and Khanna (1977), attempted to "rescue" the indigenous traditions from the West's moralism and sexual obsession (McDermott & Kripal 2003, 7). Kinsley's approach, involving historical, textual, and field-based studies came from the Cold War, a world divided, and the need to understand other cultures in depth. Other approaches include that of Gatwood (1985), who places Kali in a typology of Hindu goddesses, where some are milder, "wives" to gods, like Laksmi, goddess of wealth and well-being. Others like Kali, who belongs to the category of Sakti goddesses, maybe more martial, and independent of male consorts.

McDermott and Kripal conclude their introduction with the observation that while "dissonances" between Western and South Asian understanding of Kali exist, if anything her complexity has been enhanced and she has not been "demonized" or made extreme (9–10).[6] Western scholars of Kali "write within a long discursive history richly troubled and amply inspired by a whole host of genres and personalities" (9), with interpretations drawing from their own intellectual and hermeneutic traditions, such as those of psychoanalysis and feminism. For example, Caldwell, in a feminist reading, associates the goddess with tribal women at the margins of society, as "insider," in contrast with a Kali who has been coopted by Brahmanical and male-dominant thinking (in McDermott & Kripal 2003). McDermott's essay on Kali on the Internet in this volume describes the perception by the Hindu diaspora in the West of feminists and New Age[7] proponents of Kali as neocolonialists.[8] Kripal offers a psychoanalytic perspective, where, in Hinduism the world is a show, hidden from our ego-centered and limited understanding. Tantra (of the left-handed kind) aims to expand human consciousness beyond convention, where the Tantric "hero" works to transcend his ego/self, and becomes the goddess and is transformed (2003, 196).[9] Kripal discusses a history of

Kali in the psychoanalytic tradition,[10] beginning with Freud's argument against Romain Rolland, the French mystic and biographer of Kali's saint Ramakrishna. Freud's own stand against the "illusions of religion" (Kripal 2003, 198) was posited as "an oceanic feeling" by Rolland in 1927, referring to the saint's many mystical experiences. Freud, says Kripal, saw the oceanic experience as the psychic regression to the infant's unitive state. In this tradition of scholarship on Kali the mother goddess embodies psychological patterns based in Indian child-rearing practices and Brahmanical social values. This explains why Tantric ritual divides women into mother, and a sexually threatening lover, and why spiritual and sexual energies are synthesized in Tantric belief and ritual.[11]

Diana Eck, observing Kali's bloodied image at Kalighat Temple in Kolkata admits that she initially found the goddess to be "repulsive," but comments that her worshipers do not appear to be fearful. Where divine power claims both life and death, a "flowering and finality," there is something "profoundly true," Eck observes, in such a violent image (2003, 142–143). In deeply moving words, as she describes her visit to a morgue in Mexico where her brother's tortured and battered body lies, Eck compares the concept of Sakti to the Christian Holy Spirit, which she sees as feminine, and which comforts as it "hovered with immense wingspan over us" (143).

My participants comment on the enormity that is Sakti, uncontainable, and inexplicable. Like its embodied and iconic representation in Kali, Sakti gives life, and deals death, for its own reasons, beyond human comprehension. Kinsley, in his phenomenological interpretation of Kali in text and over changes to her meaning in different streams of thought over time, is insightful, as he observes that the "Hindu apprehension of the divine" is one that is complex, and inexhaustible, and cannot be circumscribed. Yet this apprehension is "ultimately redeeming" to he who sees beyond Kali's fearsome exterior (1975a, 2–3). Kali changes, but continues to point to "certain fundamental truths" in Hindu religious and philosophical traditions (5). While Kali also undergoes changes in how she is represented in iconic appearance over time in relation to the different sectarian streams, again, what is essential to her remains unchanged, adding dimension to those traditions (86). Thus, Kali moves over the centuries from the "helper" of the goddess Durga in their epic battle against demons (in the sixth-century CE text, the *Devi-Mahatmya*), to a goddess subdued, as she dances out of control, by the god Siva, to one who is simultaneously terrifying and death-dealing even as she is smiling, young, beautiful, offering the boon of salvation, and liberating the dedicated aspirant from fear of death (114). Kinsley concludes that Bengali Sakta devotionalism in the songs of Ramprasad Sen (1718–1975) and Kali's own devotee and saint, Ramakrishna (1836–1886), "completes" and "tames" this once-wild and terrifying deity.[12] She is now the Mother, compassionate and caring, who grants her grace to her "children" (116–117) who takes that child, devoid of ego, here the supplicant, on her lap.[13]

Kali *is* her created world (she is immanent in it), and simultaneously *maya*, "illusion" or attachment to the world that blinds us from seeing it as only a "contingent reality" (134). The devotee or adept who penetrates that illusion rises above fear of flux, change, and death (of the ego/self), and perceives that which is permanent and eternal. Kali's sword severs ignorance, offers release and a perception of a larger reality of which creation is merely a part. This, says Kinsley, is Kali's paradox—she is the flux of nature, the flow of things, as well as ultimate stasis (137)—the Mother's lap the devotee aspires to reach, the boon of salvation she grants. Kinsley concludes with the observation that over her history Kali is "tamed" or "completed" by the Tantric hero's efforts to really see who is, by the childlike devotion of her "children" Ramprasad and Ramakrishna, and "softened" from her earlier demon-slaying persona (and fearsome iconic appearance) in myth. Her "taming" does not detract from the Hindu vision of the divine but rather reinforces and enriches it (149).

In the accounts I present, for Kali's devotees their mother Kali is indeed that compassionate power that protects, and shelters from life's storms. But I would not find in their accounts any notion that she is "tamed," even where Kali offers glimpses of her grace in life's exigencies. Like Sakti, she is an unpredictable "force." The grace she dispenses is not a given—even to the devoted. She is difficult to comprehend, to take for granted, even dangerous. Participants spoke of the risks involved in performing her rituals at home and that these had to be done just right not to incur the wrath of the deity. Kali's unpredictability, her "difficult" nature would on occasion be interpreted as a mother's moral authority to be stern, to guide a wayward offspring, but not to explain herself—if a mother is punishing, her ways are those of love.[14] One male participant described this as "the many faces of a woman." So, he said, there is one face when she goes to the cinema, another when she admonishes her child. The salvation Kali offers her "child" is described by Bani, a female participant, as her "coming to realize Kali's true meaning." She described this place, even in life, as a "holiday," a time to rest, like the mother's lap sought by Kali's poets. Another participant would describe this "glimpse," anubhuti, as one where he saw his "true self," atman. Alokebabu, Kali's priest and Tantric adept, asked rhetorically, "When I die, who [inhabited] that body? Who *am* "I?" Each referred, in different words, to that original nonduality of divinity, to stasis and stillness, transcendent of life's flux.

Kinsley introductory comment is especially pertinent to the experiences I present in this book. He notes that "one must seek to discern the visionary aspect of a religious phenomenon, one that legitimates it as a religious thing. This means going beyond, or behind, the obvious social, psychic, or economic significance or function of a given phenomenon to grasp what the thing reveals to religious man, what the phenomenon reveals to man about that "other" realm of the sacred." This calls for a willingness to be open to possibilities beyond the ordinary, "to marvel and delight in the extraordinary" (1975a, 4). In Footnote 4 Kinsley explains what he means: "Visions are things that enable man to see—to see things as they really are . . . beyond the immediately sensed world . . . Visions are . . . glimpses of something other that is ultimately meaningful to man" (4).

My participants, in the accounts they shared with me in response to my central query, "How do you understand the Mother Kali?" drew on mythology (in texts like the *Devi-Mahatmya*), their understanding of concepts of Sakti as divine "force," and from how they understood devotion itself, as bhakti, in emotion and action. The many kinds of experiences they speak of in the accounts to follow in part II are described as "insight, intuitive perception," anubhuti, sudden and momentary glimpses of some larger reality—which they describe as "true," *satya*. They do not doubt the validity of revelatory knowledge, of the possibility of the miraculous, in contemporary times. Thus, within an *indigenous* epistemological paradigm that draws from different discourses, Kali's Bengali devotees speak not only to how they perceive this difficult goddess in life (in "real" ways), but also to the human-divine relationship—the greater reality, the larger truth. In such insights into the mysterious and "miraculous" workings of divinity in human lives a devotee's efforts are affirmed, inspiring spiritual growth and self-transformation. In their own voices and in the circumstances of their lives, my participants offer their own and inner understanding of Kali.

NOTES

1. McDermott and Kripal (2003), 4. See also Foulston and Abbott, referring to Kali: "In no other goddess are there found such striking polarities of character and so many symbols that point towards the totality of ultimate reality," (2009, 39).

2. On the concept of the Brahman, that Ultimate Reality from which all emanates, and which "encompasses all that we see and all that we do not see" (Foulston and Abbott, op. cit., 12).

3. Referring to the emergence of a "theistic standpoint" in the *Puranas*, which present in myths the supremacy of particular gods while simultaneously identifying them as the Brahman's manifestation, Foulston & Abbott note the supremacy of the divine feminine in Puranic texts like the *Devi-Mahatmya* in the *Markendeya Purana*, and the *Devi Bhagabat Purana*. Goddesses are associated with not only Sakti, as "power," but also primordial matter, the stuff of the created universe (*prakrti*), and illusion (maya) (op. cit., 11).

4. The Self is the Atman, to which the individual self (*atman*) aspires to return, a concept I would find expressed in the words of Alokebabu, and a participant, Dinu. Foulston and Abbott cite the *Chandyogya Upanisad*, 3.14.4: "On departing from here after death, I will become that" (op. cit., 10).

5. See also Kinsley (1975b, 1982, 1986); MacKenzie Brown (1985).

6. McDermott also notes that Indian interpretations have, on occasion, corroborated Western ones. Late nineteenth-century reformers like Raja Ram Mohan Roy saw Kali and her rituals as culturally decadent, even as the nationalist movement proposed idealized notions of female spirituality and domesticity in an independent nation, in contrast to the independence associated with Kali (1996, 295).

7. "The most recent hermeneutical layer" in the goddess' history is attributed to New Age authors (McDermott & Kripal 2003, 5). Where New Age proponents have connected powerful goddesses to matriarchal societies, McDermott correctly observes that this has been disproven, and that there is no relation between goddess imagery and an elevated status for women (McDermott 1996, 296).

8. In an earlier work, McDermott offers a survey and critique of women's writing on Kali, as a feminist icon, a symbol of female wholeness which has been "degraded" to dualities through the "willful intervention of patriarchy"(1996, 299). This calls for reclaiming those opposites from patriarchal suppression where the goddess is in fact a "a symbol of wholeness and healing, associated with repressed female power and sexuality" (293–294). However, in Indian feminist literature, the use of Kali imagery is rare, even as the goddess gives her name to a feminist publishing house, Kali for Women (296). (See also Hiltbeitel & Erndl, eds. 2000).

9. My participants would tell me that to understand Kali, one would have to "dress like her," that is, become her.

10. "Psychoanalysis is the Western hermeneutical tradition that has given the longest and most studied attention to Kali" (Kripal 2003, 13).

11. In his early and seminal work on Kali Kinsley argues against psychoanalytic interpretations, such as those by Erich Neumann (1963) and Heinrich Zimmer (1955) as "parochial, Western, male chauvinist myth" of the individual who successfully asserts his ego against a dominating mother (1975a, 130–131). While these offer some perspective on Kali's ambiguity, Kinsley argues that to see the redemptive aspects of devotion as regressive (as with Ramakrishna) is to see this saint as "misguided and deluded," and is a reductionist interpretation (132).

12. Kinsley suggests that other perspectives including nationalist (Kali as the Bengali motherland in literature), her association with epidemics, or unruly weather are not adequate in interpreting this goddess (1975a, 127–129).

13. Kinsley translates this soteriological theme that runs through Ramprasad's songs as "arms." The Bengali "*kole*" is accurately "lap" and a common metaphor, even colloquially, for ultimate "shelter," and the peace afforded by a mother's protection.

14. On a woman's moral authority as embedded in the blood with which she nourishes her unborn child, see Inden and Nicholas (1977); See also Samanta (1992b).

Chapter 2

Indigenous Epistemology

Revelatory Knowledge as Valid

It is perhaps not surprising to find the pervasiveness of miraculous experiences even into contemporary times among my participants given centuries-old philosophical traditions on the Indian sub-continent which hold that such experience has epistemological validity.[1] I begin this chapter with a brief commentary, drawing from scholarship, on the recognition of "other" ways of knowing, and the cultural parameters of such knowing. The second section presents and discusses indigenous concepts such as "intuitive insight," anubhuti, the locus of such insight, the "heart/mind," *man*, the connection between "insight" and experience with "devotion," "bhakti," and reflection and "remembering," smrti. These are concepts which have philosophical underpinnings, and I discuss these different and intertwined discourses which provide the paradigm by which my participants interpreted their experiences of Kali. In the third section of this chapter I present an evening's conversation with a group of Kali's devotees.

"VERIDICAL KNOWLEDGE" IN INDIAN PHILOSOPHICAL THOUGHT

The aura of factuality of "intuitive insight," often immediate and unsought in Kali devotees' narratives, is supported at a meta-level of discourse, where such a way of "knowing" is seen as ontologically valid in Indian philosophical thought. Matilal argues for the "rational presentation of some of the philosophical doctrines of India that are usually associated with mysticism: Advaita Vedanta and Mahayana Buddhism" (1977, 4), in a difficult language, Sanskrit, which requires years of formal study. These early philosophers, trained in logical argument, produced texts that questioned what lay beyond our everyday perceptions, but were not "rhapsodies of mystical experience" (7). They were, rather, says Matilal, a reasoned argument for mysticism as another kind of knowing (6): "[a]ll great religions contain a belief that people can be better than they are as well as a belief that people can experience more than they do" (31). Citing the second-century CE Buddhist philosopher Nagarjuna, Matilal, like Kinsley (1975a), describes two levels of reality, the everyday or "conventional" (27), and the ultimate, where the former is contingent on the latter, as "liberation," *nirvana* (27).

In his Foreword to the proceedings of a seminar on Eastern and Western concepts of knowledge Dasgupta (1995) comments on Swami Vivekananda's theory of knowledge as one which rejects the Kantian idea that reason is the only way we know. The Swami observes that the "Indian mind" is more concerned with ignorance which must be dispelled (vi). Where Kant uses reason to conclude that the "thing in itself" is unknown and unknowable, the Indian philosophical tradition finds something "higher," a "state of mind that transcends reason" (ii). Swami Vivekananda, in fact, noted that religion is beyond reasoning and not on the plane of intellect, and that which points to such knowledge is "inspiration" (analogous to anubhuti). While reason affords access to the knowledge we acquire in scientific endeavors, religious "knowing" involves realization. This is different to, and transcendent of our life of the senses, which reason and science more appropriately explain (ii). However, such realization is not possible without having lived a moral life.[2]

Swami Atmarupanananda, another contributor to this symposium, makes the point that "cultural presuppositions" determine both religious experience, and how it is expressed and interpreted. Such assumptions, emanating from a particular worldview, determine our sense of time, space, and self, as prior to experience, and are not chosen consciously—or are even debatable, but, rather, a given (1995, 20). Such presuppositions, including the mythical foundations of a culture, influence, in the larger sense, how we know (22). Comparing West with East, this author observes that in the Western humanist tradition, man is at the center, and the measure of all things, and his power to know and to reason is "deified" (29). Western self-confidence and passion for intellectual understanding is to be understood in this context, as is Western zeal for adventure, conquest and expansion (29). The Judeo-Christian concept of Time as linear, for example, says this author, sees history as progressive, leading toward fulfillment where the righteous are rewarded (27). The Hindu, on the other hand, experiences temporal fulfillment, but his long-term goal, "liberation" as *moksa* (or nirvana, in Buddhist thought, or Kali's "lap"), ultimately transcends linear Time (30). The Hindu self or atman, unlike the Christian self, simply *is*—it is not created, or dependent on divinity (e.g., Jesus) for salvation (28). The person *is* a soul (self/atman) to start with, and *has* a body, in contrast to the Christian self, which reverses these. Thus, the

Hindu, with his intrinsically pure self/soul, "gives up" his body at death, but the atman remains (to be reborn).

Hence, Bhattacharya proposes, such presuppositions change the nature of experience itself: "Different views of time cause us to experience time differently, and thereby to experience events—all of which take place in time—differently" (31). The Hindu seeks to know the truth about the soul/atman that *he* (or she) is. Atmarupananda continues on this theme, warning against "radical postmodernist perspectivism" (38) by concluding that no cultural perspective (including the Christian one) is absolute. Rather, he asserts that many paths lead to the truth (in Ramakrishna's words, often quoted by my participants). Each path, in the Vedanta, is a "partial view" of that (universal and ultimate) truth (39), like Kinsley's "contingent reality" (1975a, 134). Like Bhattacharya, this author concludes that such cultural presuppositions affect how the experiencer interprets his experience (40).

"Logical arguments are useful for they illuminate the mystical instead of deepening its mystery. In fact, the logical is indispensable . . . for the illumination of the mystical," Matilal observes (1977, 24). Kali's devotees described their experiences to me logically, in language, which took different structures in the telling. A theme of "not knowing" runs implicitly or explicitly through the accounts. At heart is the mystery of Sakti, where "experiences" afforded an intimation or insight, anubhuti, into some larger reality, beyond the everyday, truth writ large. At the same time, many observed that "there was no logic" to really understand such experiences. The central interpretive concept for experiences was the "play" of Sakti, inexplicable, and fortuitous. These comments find expression in textual traditions. Avalon notes that Sakta doctrine, like Vedanta, is a theology based on revelation, or "super-sensual experience" like the *Vedas* (1978, 30). The basis of such "knowing" is, as sense, or super-sense, "actual experience" (30–31). Partial experience is "knowing" in time and space, while supreme experience, as with the revealed texts, the *Veda*s, is the "full experience" (33).[3] Cultural presuppositions, thus, offer a context for the interpretation of the miraculous, alaukik, for Kali's devotees.

BHAKTI, ANUBHUTI, MAN, SMRTI

Most of my participants described themselves as bhaktas of the mother Kali, a word that connotes both devotee and worshiper. This is distinguished from sadhak, the "adept," whose spiritual practices and status are considered to be of a higher stature, exemplified by a person such as Alokebabu. A bhakta could come to be one because of a family's tradition and history, a personal experience leading to a love for and relationship with the deity, and translated into action as ritual worship. Such action could range from visits to the

Temple, worship at his or her home altar, or on festive days, quiet meditation, some or all of these, as a matter of personal choice.

Hawley, describing the pervasive prevalence of Bhakti as "India's true religion," and a religion of the "heart" beyond organized religion, observes that the number of deities is secondary. What is primary is the social connectedness, a religion of community participation, song, enthusiasm, but also personal challenge (2015, 4). Bhakti implies direct encounter with the divine, and is *experienced* in the lives of individual people (2). The concept is a derivative of the Sanskrit root *bhaj*, "devotion, trust, worship, love" (in Hindi and in Bengali). Bhaj also means being a part [of], that which belongs to or is contained in anything (Monier-Williams 1964). Hawley adds that such "sharing" also points to "god," *bhagaban*, the deity who shares, even as the concept extends to fellow devotees (2015, 5). Prentiss interprets this term to mean "partake, participate," signifying the devotee's relationship with the deity, "participating" in (her) by singing of her, and saying her name (1999, 24). Moreover, bhakti is not one single thing (Hawley, op. cit., 5) and diverse in its expression. Yet, as he notes and I would find, there is a cohesive theme in bhakti's many expressions, here in experience and in ritual practice. Centrally, the paradigm in Bhakti idiom is that of love (Carman 1982, 127; McDaniel 1989, 3; Ramanujan 1982), and involves establishing a reciprocal connection between deity and devotee in terms of a generally hierarchical human relationship, such as that of master-servant (the god Rama and Hanuman), mother and child in the case of Kali, though that between lovers like Krsna and Radha is questionably more egalitarian. The deity is made flesh, embodied (Prentiss op. cit., 41), and the relationship between devotee and deity is, thus, a personal and powerfully emotional one. However, bhakti involves a love (inclusive of trust, respect, and faith) from one younger toward an older person, a child for a parent, a disciple for a guru (or student for teacher), or a devotee for the deity. A young female participant, Srimonti, noted that the bhakti she feels for her parents is different to the love she feels for her younger siblings.[4] Alokebabu would expand on Bhakti by distinguishing the simple love of a child for its mother from one where establishing such a relationship required effort. The divinity must be *claimed* by the power of the devotee's love and devotion, he said.

Debu, a man in his early fifties and a *sebayet* (ritual caretaker) at Kalighat Temple, added dimension to bhakti in a concept which would find frequent expression in my participants' accounts of religious experience. He described any relationship, whether of family, of friendship, or business, as "connection," *samparka*. At one level the mother Kali is understood, and experienced by normative measures of motherhood in Bengali culture—in her compassion and as protective presence but also as a moral, stern, and guiding force in the lives of her "children." Debu illustrated this to me in mundane terms, where a woman, as mother, has different facets to her, stern, tender, caring, in relating to her children. But at the heart of such connection is our *experience* of a person, he added, is how we *really* know him or her. So it is with the mother Kali, he said, that we come to *know* what she truly means by *experiencing* her as mother. Debu described this "knowing" as anubhuti, yielded to her devotees in glimpses of intuitive insight as the true essence of divinity.

Anubhuti (n.), as concept, transcends this mundane understanding of the devotee-deity relationship as one of child and mother. It is related to the verb phrase, "to experience," *anubhab kara*, which can include perception, realization, and intuition (Monier-Williams 1964), but also "feeling." The hard work involved in a relationship of bhakti yields results—a child healed, lost jewelry found, mobile lights without observable source, precognitive dreams, and more—anubhuti, granted by the grace of the Mother Kali, and the wondrous workings of that larger truth she embodies, Sakti. Bani would explain anubhuti as an experience achieved by dedicated effort, where faith is then reinforced by that experience, or several experiences—intuitive, unmediated, and immediate knowledge (veridical, in Indian philosophical discourse), and transformative of a person. Anubhuti might inspire a person to begin his or her religious journey in what such experience suggests of possibilities, or affirm faith already there. Anubhuti is subjective and personal experience. A priest conducting the annual worship for the goddess Durga also described such experience to me as different at different levels for different people, and that spiritual discipline and practice, as well as a person's religious environment could be conducive to such experiences. However, he noted, for the spiritually advanced ritual and environment could become unnecessary. At this spiritual level, anubhuti is transcendent of book learning or logic, an ineffable experience, as many Kali devotees asserted. My participants described anubhuti as "real" (*asal*) because personally experienced. The words "true events," *satya ghatana,* would sometimes follow such "real" experiences. Their accounts were often emotionally recounted, suggesting how deeply moved they were by what such experience implied.

Sri Rabindra Mohan Roy explained anubhuti as "feelings" [*sic*], where the "glassness" of glass, or the "woodness" of wood could not be communicated, even though glass and wood were palpable. Dinu, Bani's husband, who ran a small pharmaceutical store and whom we will meet later, explained anubhuti by lighting a candle on the dining table at which we were seated in their home in southern Kolkata. "If the windows were closed," he said, the flame would be upright and still." I asked him to explain further. If the smoke from incense sticks goes straight up, without interference (from a breeze), its stillness, he explained, is anubhuti. Such an explanation appears to be analogous with other themes and religious concepts in Hindu belief, such as the child seeking and finally finding shelter on the mother Kali's lap, of liberation from cycles of rebirth and final stasis, and the return to stasis, oneness, and nonduality. Anubhuti is that insight into a transcendent truth.

The "heart/mind," *man*, was, in devotees' discourse, the locus of devotion, bhakti, and of anubhuti, as well as where "experience" was reflected upon, and "remembered" as smrti. Indian philosophical discourse distinguishes between the "subtle body," *suksma sarira*, distinct from the outer or "gross body," *sthula sarira*. The former's components are the powers of perception and discrimination (*buddhi*), consciousness of self (*ahamkara*), reason (*citta*), and the *man*. The "subtle body" is mobile, and unlimited by time and space, unlike the "gross body" which lives in time and space, and perishes. Merits and demerits are "deposited" in the "subtle body" over a life (or over many lives). It is unbounded and capable of rebirth in other "gross bodies." The mobility of the "subtle body" accounts for the extra-physical experiences of a yogi, for example, who can move this faculty out of his body at will (Monier-Williams 1963; Potter 1977, 94; Sinha 1966, 1969).

The *man* is the faculty that responds to the outer world (Sinha 1969). Where the Atman (Self, writ large) is unknowable and cannot itself be known (Revathy 2004, 335), the *man*, itself insentient, and the passive recipient of knowledge, becomes the conduit for knowing (338). The *man* works with the senses, comprehends objects, perceives, and learns (339). As such, it is "always active" and the locus of emotion, faith, doubt, intent, desire, as well as intellect, and reflection.[5] It is also, as a faculty that is easily distracted, where ego blinds the self/atman/knower to the truth that is Atman. However, the *man* can be focused, through ritual, or meditation, "a secretary" passing on information to the self (Potter 1977, 94–95; see also Monier-Williams 1963, 86–87). In a parable the "self" is described as the lord of the chariot, the "body" to the chariot, the "discriminating intellect" to the charioteer, and the *man* to the reins (in the *Katha Upanisad*, 1.3.3., cited in Coburn 1984, 161).

The *man* is the locus of both memory and the revelatory experience it remembers. "Memory," smrti, is distinguished in the Indian philosophical tradition from "revealed knowledge," *sruti*. Smrti refers to that which is remembered of revelation (Embree 1972). Sruti takes precedence in onto-logical status over smrti, since revelation is related to direct divine impera-tive—knowledge in its most pristine, veridical, and immediate form (e.g., the *Vedas*). Smrti involves remembering, and recording (in early Hindu law and jurisprudence, for example, the text *Manusmrti*).[6] However, the status of smrti is also debated. While the Jaina school of philosophy holds that it is another source of non-perceptual knowledge, to Nyayayika and Buddhist philosophers "valid" knowledge is defined as veridical experience, a first-time cognitive event as sruti. Smrti merely records and repeats this original experience, and, in its reinterpretation of that original experience, and in synthesizing that experience with other such experiences, is constructed, and possibly inaccurately so.[7] From an epistemological viewpoint smrti thus ranks lower than sruti. So books of law, like *Manusmrti*, are seen to depend on the *Vedas* for authoritativeness, and are not in themselves sources of knowledge or authorities in their own right (Matilal 1986; Potter 1977; Sinha 1969).

For my participants, anubhuti as "experiences" have as their locus the *man*, a term which appeared in a multiplicity of contexts in accounts I would hear. This faculty is where their experiences are remembered and recollected as smrti. Any close, tender relationship is described by my participants as essentially a "weakness of the *man*," *maner durbbalata*. An open-hearted laugh is described as a "laugh from the *man*" and to be able to confide one's troubles lightens the *man*. Faith is born and felt here, as is devotion, bhakti. The guru or deity may use the *man* as channel to "pull" at or communicate with the devotee (*maner tan*). It has unuttered "secret words" (*maner katha*), which may be "heard" by the guru as he "intuits" the spiritual potential of the disciple before he initiates him or her. The *man* may be "opened," making it receptive to such communication, while a restless *man* cannot hear the call of the guru (or deity). A crisis especially focuses the *man* upon divinity as it urgently supplicates that power for succor, and its call is particularly effective at such a time. The *man* can be "brought to stillness," *manke sthir kara*. It is through the *man* that a miracle, of whatever sort, is first perceived (or "received") as communication. The *man* is where anubhuti, as communication, are interpreted. The *man* is a listening faculty as well as a seeing one. It is located "inside" oneself, and integral to that self. The *man* is where thought, joy,[8] sorrow, and longing are experienced, and where that which lies beyond everyday experience is intuited—as anubhuti. Its journey, over many lives, to stillness, to Kali's lap, to liberation from rebirth is described as the "rites of the mind," *maner samskar*.

The *man* is also the repository of smrti, remembrance and recollection, ordering the experiences of a lifetime in an integrated web of meaning where each event has relevance and meaning within the larger story of a life. It is in the recollection of anubhuti, variously, that the devotee comes to intimate some larger truth, including that of the atman/self, who he or she truly is in the larger scheme of things, impelling spiritual growth, a becoming. Bani would describe my recording of her recollected spiritual "journey" as smrti. The *man* then is the locus of spiritual transformation for the person. Anubhuti, insight into divine workings, initially move the *man* to wonder, to question, and to act. Subsequent experiences, should these occur, sustain and strengthen it. However, the stories told to me by Kali's devotees obviously cannot speak of the ultimate, a return to the beginning. They do, however, speak of closures achieved as well as intimated along the way.

KALI DEVOTEES ON ANUBHUTI, SAKTI/SAKTI, AND BHAKTI: AN EVENING'S CONVERSATION

The following conversation I had with five men one evening during my first phase of research illustrates the views of some Kali devotees, (to whom I had been introduced by Alokebabu). They ranged in age from their forties to sixties, small business owners (Biswajit, Probir, and Tarun, Biswajit's uncle); a retired officer who had worked in a steel firm, (Goswami); and two retired musicians (Santosh, Ananda). We met at Biswajit's home, in the vicinity of Kalighat Temple. I asked how they understood the accounts of experiences I had heard from other worshipers. The men offered different responses to my questions.

Goswami, who had been initiated by Alokebabu and called him his guru, recalled that he "remembered" Kali's saint Ramakrishna in his *man* when he faced financial troubles related to his daughter's marriage, and "got results," that is, his troubles were resolved. Many anubhuti have protected him from danger, he said, and have brought him peace: "When I have such anubhuti, my *man* is attracted to Ma Kali."

Debu, the Temple caretaker, described bhakti as the "desire," *anurag*, to know the deity, a matter of effort and interest. If one is not interested, the question of knowing what devotion means does not arise. Probir, following on from Debu's comment, also observed that effort is central to bhakti, and that "it is not enough to sit about." He recounted his experience, how, when suffering from a brain tumor caused by a head injury in an accident, he went to see his guru: "My guru touched my head when I went for my second surgery. He said, 'Go, you will be well.' If I had not received that sakti, I would have died." His guru had acquired his powers by effort, was the implication here.

Santosh commented that it was sakti (as human capacity) that impelled any effort—toward the larger end. It was his passion to improve his skills as a musician, and it was his single-minded focus in practice which created sakti in him. This sakti/Sakti found expression as his ability to bring out the "essence," *bhava*, of the musical scale. I asked, did he understand his dedication to music as bhakti. In answer to my question, Santosh, who prefaced his reply by saying that he saw Alokebabu as his guru, drew parallels between his musical and religious practice. Both involved "discipline," *sadhana*, which implied bhakti, and sakti, here as capacity.

When I asked if my research project could be considered an act of bhakti Goswami commented, if done with dedication, and selflessly, it could be seen as sadhana, disciplined effort, integral to bhakti. "Kali," he said, "has woken this anubhuti in you, and it is 'real,' asal. But you must be committed and surrender yourself to your labor, or you won't reach your goal. See Kali in your *man*, understand her Sakti, for you to find the sakti to do this work." He also observed that my "path" might traverse many lives, and concluded that Kali had "brought [me] here [to do this work]." Biswajit, also emphasizing the centrality of disinterested effort, suggested that "good work" (*sukrti*) in a previous life had dictated my choice in this one. The devotee, he said, has to work to understand Ma Kali, but, "for whom you work, she will take you on her lap, this is the greatest peace. Her darkness is 'gentle,' *snigdha*, 'merciful,' *dayamayi*, and 'compassionate,' *karunamayi*." My initial inspiration, anubhuti, to proceed on this "path" to understand Kali, the men proposed, required great effort to get to that point.

In the narratives I present in the second part of this book my participants "interpret" their anubhuti, "experiences" in their various forms and in different contexts, in terms of interrelated concepts. Their own believing, questioning, recollecting, and loving *man* is at the core of such interpretation. Bhakti, as flexible concept, emerges within relationships (with deity, or the guru, or with family), and in action, in musical practice, or in a research project. The power to work steadfastly, with discipline and dedication, needs sakti, and is bhakti. Anubhuti as "insight," fortuitous, unsolicited, and ultimately inexplicable, inspires my research project, in their view, but also can be understood as the transfer of sakti from guru to disciple, and healing a brain tumor. Anubhuti, as such "experiences," are both real (asal), and true (satya). Kali's devotees are moved to wonder, and to interpret as best they can the mysteries to which they have been given a brief glimpse. In the remembering and in the telling, they are moved and transformed by those intimations.

NOTES

1. See Kakar, on the "greater acceptance" of psychic phenomena in South Asia. He also notes that in the indigenous medical system, Ayurveda, dreams are connected with psychic life and clairvoyance (1982, 181, 246).

2. In the same volume, Bhattacharya, commenting on "valid cognition" (*prama*) in the school of Advaita Vedanta thought, notes the different levels of spiritual competence which allow for a knowledge of the ultimate as Atman or Brahman (1995, 83–84).

3. Avalon describes Sakti as Time and Space, the source of change, and change itself (1978, 28). Kinsley describes Sakti as a protective aspect of the goddess, a positive force, which provokes creative activity (1989, 12–13). In a later essay Kinsley describes Sakti as action, play, dance, power, and might (1996, 83).

4. The love and affection for someone younger to oneself is *sneha*.

5. Monier-Williams describes derivatives from the base term *man* as ranging in meaning from the affective to the cognitive, where the mind is the faculty of imagination, as well as of desire, affections, and mental suffering (1964).

6. The *Manusmrti* was written by several authors, over centuries, and is generally dated to the turn of the first millennium.

7. "Memory-experience was never regarded by any non-Jaina philosopher (a Naiyayika or a Buddhist) to constitute a piece of knowledge, a *prama*, a cognitive awareness which amounts to truth" (Matilal 1985, 262).

8. Participants use the Bengali word *ananda*, a concept that Sri Rabindra Mohan Roy would tell me is more than happiness, which is a sensory state. Its connotation in a religious context suggests a state closer to "bliss," an experience that is shared, and transcendent.

Chapter 3

On Narrative

Autobiographical Recollection, Interpreting the Miraculous Experience

Scholars in recent studies question Western positivism that disallows ways of knowing and being which cannot be scientifically proven (Kripal 2010; Obeyesekere 2012; Presti 2018; Raj & Dempsey 2008). While Kripal notes the presence of the paranormal even in the contemporary West, Obeyesekere, and Raj and Dempsey argue for recognizing (in social science scholarship) the pervasiveness of the "miraculous" in South Asian cultures. In this chapter I frame the narratives I will present in part II of this book by discussing scholarly commentary on narrative itself, specifically autobiographical narrative, and how this relates to the expression of "experience"; on "other" ways of knowing as valid and how such "knowing" can be expressed and understood; and, in conclusion, briefly comment on both type and content of the narratives of experience to follow as well as how autobiographical recollection and expression of "experience" can be interpreted and understood in a cultural context (Geertz 1986; Turner & Edward Bruner 1986).

EXPERIENCE, RECOLLECTION, AND NARRATIVE

A body of scholarship observes that the expression of human experience (in narrative, art, and song) is amenable to cultural analysis in terms of social values and conceptions of personhood and gender (Appadurai et al. 1991; Smith 1991; Turner & Edward Bruner 1986). Murray notes that "narrative" itself can be diverse—as episodic, interpretive, and selective—especially when such narratives emerge in the context of an unstructured interview, or in conversation between ethnographer and participants (2018). Narrative, he continues, expresses agency and transformation, and that as such it can be empowering, liberating, and life-affirming, as it arranges experience, in longer or shorter, "episodic" stories (Murray 2018, 264–265, 269–270).[1] This has been proposed in earlier scholarship suggesting that the process of recollection in autobiographical narrative is an imaginative undertaking constitutive of a sense of self and cultural identity (Jerome Bruner 1987; Johnson 1991).

Three related and central issues emerge within an anthropological approach to human experience generally, and its expression. Victor Turner distinguishes "an experience" from "*mere* experience." Where the latter "is simply the passive endurance and acceptance of events," *an* experience "stands out from the evenness of passing hours and years and forms a "structure of experience" (Turner 1986, 35). Geertz suggests that the anthropology of "experience" is a study of the use of artifice, of reconstruction, where a past event is reinvented in its expression and retelling: "[e]xperiences, like tales, fetes, potteries, rites, dramas . . . memoirs, ethnographies . . . are made" (Geertz 1986, 380). Abrahams, expressing a similar view to Turner and Geertz, notes that events (as experiences rather than "experience") and their interpretive recollection within culturally shared cognitive and affective categories in a cultural community properly outline a life. The anthropologist's task, he says, is, on the one hand, an emic one of eliciting the indigenous exegesis of experiences and their relationship to concepts of selfhood. On the other hand, it is an etic enterprise in attempting to "effectively convey the idea of experience in any culture" (Abrahams 1986, 57).

These themes that "experiences" structure "experience"; that experiences are reconstructed in the recollection of a life; and that such expression is situated within a cultural and collective context are broadly and variously reiterated in scholarship on the processes of memory in autobiographical narrative. Distinguishing recollection from mere remembering, a "constructivist" approach holds that recollection is actively selective and imaginative, and may be culturally and temporally situated when expressed in the story of a life. Within such a process forgetting (or deliberate omission) is also selective (Kuchler & Melion 1991; Johnson 1991). In a cinematic analogy certain remembered images are picked on, involving primarily sensory experiences—visual, auditory, olfactory, spatial, and temporal, as well as related feelings and moods. These selected images, moods, and feelings are organized, giving meaning and coherence to the past. The recollection of a life's events, then, is one that is constructed, or reconstructed, essentially an "artifice" (Crites 1971, 294). Such narrative organizes experience, "endowing it with meaning" (Narayan 1989, 243), "laying down routes into memory . . . not only guiding the life narrative up to the present but also directing it into the future" (Jerome Bruner 1987, 31).

Recollection, by this definition, involves an act of the imagination, an aesthetic undertaking and achievement. An autobiographical account is a *story* of a life (or some aspect of it), constructed or fashioned out of selected material. It is an active interpretation of the past, rather than simply a retrieval of "facts" from memory, a "long route" to meaning (Narayan 1989, 100). This selective and interpretive process is essentially episodic. To be selected, each episode or event must be meaningful to the person recounting it. That is, it must also be integral to the larger story, the wider context—that of the narrator's life. In other words, the remembered episode must be of some significance to be included in a (continuing) life-story—in its implications at the time of occurrence (the past), for the then-future, the narrator's present. Imagination, then, draws from intellect as well as from emotion as it recollects "life facts" as a metaphor. It entails an insight into similarities and continuities between different aspects of experience, finding the universal in the particular, and revelatory of essential truths about a life. Warnock observes:

> For the creative construction of a story involves seeking out what is significant, what is to feature as part of the plot. When we re-live something in recollection, experiencing again what it was like, we are discovering a truth; and truth, even if it is a truth concerning ourselves, is necessarily in one sense general (1987, 132).

Such a realization is integral to a sense of personal continuity, a coherent and integrated sense of self over time, as well as the placement of that self in a wider scheme of things, among more general, even transcendental truths. Imaginative insight, then, involves more than individual perceptions and recollection involves more than the merely private and idiosyncratic. Such perceptions and acts include collective processes of perception and understanding, basic to our living in a "shared, meaningful world" (Johnson 1991, 75). As a cognitive undertaking, the process of recollection is one means of transmitting "preserved symbolic meanings" (84) crucial to cultural coherence and continuity.

While at some universal level a story constituted of life-events speaks of general human conditions, such as suffering, or victory over adversity, its specifics are to be found within the narrator's unique situation in space-time. Further, both in content and style a life-story meshes within its cultural fabric—tellers and listeners share a "deep structure" about the nature of a life lived. It follows then that there is no one kind of life-story cross-culturally. As Jerome Bruner notes, a culture abides by a "criteria of rightness" on self-report. There is a "right" kind of autobiography that depends upon cultural as well as linguistic conventions, reflecting "canonical stances and circumstances," the "possible lives" in a culture (1987, 15). The self-telling of life narratives result in a "becoming" that which is recounted and told (15), a self that situates itself within its cultural reality. Further, even any one culture or community may have more than simply one kind of life-story to tell. Oral narrative, as a performative act, is contingent upon several factors, such as the intentions of the narrator, his or her awareness of appropriate styles of telling a life-story, his or her perceptions of and relationship with the listening audience (Narayan 1989, 8; Smith 1981). In other words, various personal, as well as social and cultural conditions impinge upon an oral utterance. It is implicit that such a story can assume its audience's understanding and empathy (Abrahams 1986, 60). Where orally recounted to an audience, such a narrative is contingent upon a particular encounter (here, with the ethnographer, in a particular context), with the implicit understanding that both narrator and audience will share a comprehension of the narrative's essence and true meaning. It follows, then, that there are particular ways of remembering as well, of particular "experiences" that are selected to tell of.[2]

NARRATIVE, "NONRATIONAL" EXPERIENCE, AND THE MIRACULOUS

Kripal, writing about four Western men whose works on, and experiences of the paranormal are largely unknown, observes critically that in the professional study of religion Western "academic respectability" denies "marvels" even as (Western) popular culture embraces such possibilities, "our secret in plain sight" (2010, 6).[3] Citing Schopenhauer, Kant, and Einstein, Kripal describes (everyday) space and time as illusory constructs of our minds (11). He argues that clairvoyance and precognition see the world as it really is, in contrast to our perceptions (12) and cites anthropologists like Edith Turner, Margaret Mead, and Michael Winkelman writing on their encounters with spirits, and their experiences of their own psychic abilities. He proposes the ontological basis of such "magical" phenomena in deep emotional states where human capacities are themselves not adequately understood, and the laws of nature that appear to govern our perceptions even less so. In other words, says Kripal, "magical powers are real" (13). Further, he distinguishes the physical reality of the brain from the Mind, which is "something else, something alien, something really, really weird" (268). The brain's death does not dispense with the Mind, a "program" and consciousness that continues to exist, filtered through the physical reality of the brain (264). Kripal proposes the "filter thesis," which points to the paranormal event as at once real and beyond-real, as an expression of "Mind" beyond brain.[4] The event is filtered and translated through the linguistic and cultural capacities of the (left) brain (269). Psychical and paranormal phenomena are, then, Kripal observes, in need of interpretation (not belief), as hermeneutical realities which work like texts and stories (257), where the real, the religious, and the fictional can have permeable boundaries (34):

> What is permitted to cross the threshold . . . is not only filtered, selected, and narrowed. It also comes through *in a different form*, whether this is a dream, a vision, a symbol, a text, or a drawing . . . it is *translated.* (author's italics, 257)

Obeyesekere, a cultural anthropologist who looks to both Western and Buddhist traditions, notes that reason is not the only access to knowledge as the "Cartesian cogito" proposes (2012, xii), and that he refuses to be "tied down to any epistemology of empiricism" as he addresses the "visionary experience" in his book (1). Intuitive knowing, Obeyesekere argues, is not opposed to rational knowing, rather "the very basis for Reason lies in intuitive understanding," a first principle preceding the Cartesian thinking-I ("Spinoza's God," 2–3). Describing himself a "product of two Enlightenments, the European and the Buddhist," he observes:

> One cannot live *without* Reason and one cannot live *with* it either, at least in its exclusionary Enlightenment or Euro-rational sense. Rationality for me still remains a powerful means of knowing, but I criticize here the closure of our minds to modes of knowledge, especially visionary knowledge, that bypass the cogito. . . . My ideal is the Buddha who discovered the foundations of his epistemology through meditative trance but then reworked these foundational ideas later in more rational and philosophically profound form in his discourses. (4)[5]

Countering the "myopia" of assuming that reason is the sole pathway to knowledge, Obeyesekere proposes that "intangibles" [such] as visions and dreams are phenomena worthy of investigation and description and open to theorizing (2), and that "[a]s with visions, our dreams compel us to recognize that the limits of language are *not* the limits of thought" (380). Yet, the content of dreams reflects the dreamer's culture (378), and visual experiences are, in the end, described in language (379).

An edited volume comments on the miracle as "modern conundrum" in South Asian religious traditions (Raj & Dempsey 2008). Dempsey, in her introduction, suggests a connection between Indo-European languages in the etymology of the word "miracle" from (Latin) *miraculum*, the wonder-inspiring aspect of an event, while *vismaya* is the derivative from the Sankrit root *smi*, also "wondrous event."[6] Dempsey notes that these "pervasively complex phenomena" have not been scrutinized, but rather distanced by scholars of religion in this part of the world (2008, 1).

Dempsey defines "miracle" broadly as applied to such phenomena as healings, punishments, mystical experience, and visions—in different contexts, including those associated with the powers of saints as well as divinities. Depending on the region, different terms describe such phenomena, for example, *alaukika*, "beyond [the] everyday," in Hindi (2-3). I have referred to this word earlier, in Bengali, where "*laukik*" is "this worldly," and alaukik is "other worldly." Citing Babb (1986, 176, 192), Dempsey observes that seeing the miraculous as irrational and unscientific "distorts significant realities" in the Hindu worldview (4), and that within this worldview a miraculous event is "naturally anticipated" and "lacks any element of truly radical surprise" (17).[7]

Dempsey prefers "miraculous" to "supernatural," which implies an assumption of what is "natural." Yet, as ethnography-based work by contributors to this volume illustrate, "narratives and conceptions of the miraculous . . . confound" divides of science and religion, West and the non-Western, ethnographer and native, and modern and traditional (2). Western anti-miracle views, such as those of the eighteenth-century Scottish phi-losopher David Hume, come from a post-Enlightenment scientific, empirical worldview, where miracles violate laws of nature, an "irrationality" associ-ated with "primitive," pre-modern, and colonial thinking about the "Other" (3–4). Where miracles are experiences[8] and can be the language of faith, speaking from experience in defiance of "established logic" are, in fact, "worthy of analysis," Dempsey asserts (13). Gold, in this volume, noting that miracles are "foundational" in South Asian religions, and yet have not been adequately addressed by scholars, points to a kind of Western positiv-ist imperialism that gives primacy to data which is available for academic analyses (as also noted by Kripal 2010; Obseyesekere 2012). On the one hand, such analyses risk a reductionist approach to miracles; on the other, there is a need to do them justice, without running the risk of being perceived as unscholarly (Gold 2008).

Goonasekera (in Dempsey & Raj 2008), continuing on this theme, com-ments on the conflict between Sinhala Buddhist discourses on miracles, and Western, post-Enlightenment ones, where validity depends on verifiability, or that which can be falsified (57). He refers to Max Weber's demystification as a concept that debunks pre-modern and nonmodern notions of truth on epis-temological and ontological grounds (Weber 1922). Given the "intellectual power" of the modern worldview and its globalized reach, "it is miraculous that pre-modern and the non-modern perspectives still exist, rather robustly, even in European civilization, and amazing that they continue to be the dominant perspectives in the non-European world" (58), even as South Asians may not be "unanimous" themselves about the possibility of miracles (59). Goonasekera describes miracles associated with worshipers of the god Kataragama in the context of the December 2004 tsunami, such as statues of the Virgin Mary and the Buddha that stood firm against the wave, and a man saved by a crocodile from drowning. However, he notes also that "explana-tions" by "modern" narrators, his contemporary participants, are indirect and suggested, involving questions or comments where the meaning of the experience is left to be inferred, indirectly, by one of "equal heart" (77). Here I gather the author means himself, the ethnographer.

My participants located my presence in a scheme of rebirth; my "quest" for Kali's meaning—to them—an effort that had possibly spanned many lives. Somewhere in that past, some suggested, I had perhaps been more than a devotee but rather, an "adept," sadhak, who needed to complete what had been left incomplete. I was, then, one of "equal heart," in Goonesekere's words, who would understand their experiences and how *they* understood these. There is, centrally, trust, the assumption that as fellow Bengali, a woman ("kin" to the Mother goddess), the mother of a daughter myself, that I would believe, and above all respect the experiences they shared with me. These are points I have made earlier already. In their interpretation—but not explanation—of visions and dreams they made of symbol (as Kali herself) and of concept (Sakti), that which was meaningful to them, even as they claimed that their experiences were in essence ineffable. However, and of course, they narrated their experiences in language, in this case Bengali, making our conversation particularly intimate where that sharing was evocative of cultural sharing, of ways of being. They spoke to a particular and receptive audience, myself, and answered my questions with particular, selected, and remembered accounts of the deity's intervention in their lives, but left questions, appropriately—for how do we conclusively understand the mystery that is divinity as Sakti? Experiences were "filtered" (Kripal), or "translated" (Obeyesekere), making of cultural "meaning" something deeply and personally meaningful. Bhakti, as concept, and as an emotional rather than rational relationship with the deity, provided the context for how my participants, Kali's devotees, interpreted their experiences of their deity.[9]

My participants' narratives related to different contexts of life and took different structures. The shorter, more anecdotal accounts were offered as illustration, a brief glimpse afforded a person of Kali/Sakti, moving him or her to devotion. Alokebabu, Kali's priest and guru for many of my participants, refused to talk to me about his reputed "powers," of which his disciples, my participants had told me. His "story" is elicited by me from his disciples' perceptions—and stories—about him. Such accounts are "constructive" by others, of the man.[10] It is only at the end of my second phase of research, five years after I first met him that he recounts an event, *implying* the *possible* powers he may have while still leaving these open to interpretation. Bani free-associates story after story in a long narrative of ostensibly miraculous events (as dreams, events involving gurus, even dreams within dreams), in a spiritual (but not chronological) continuity. Some longer narratives I present are simultaneously autobiographical (involving close family) and biographical (not directly about the narrator). These are chronological, clearly structured, with a beginning, a middle and an end, albeit without "logic," because without explanation, as the devotee herself notes. How divinity works in the world cannot, by definition be known conclusively. Kali/Sakti remains a mystery, and anubhuti, variously intimate at best glimpses of that mystery.

To summarize some themes from the preceding part of this chapter: the narratives related to their experience of Kali which I would hear from her devotees emerged in the specifics of a particular ethnographic encounter, within semi-structured "interviews," more accurately, conversations. They were centrally autobiographical, even when relating "an experience" (see Turner 1986) associated with a friend, more often a close relative. Whether described in brief, as illustrative of a point the narrator wished to make, or embedded in a larger and more chronological account, these recollections served to structure the larger story of the narrator's life. They were selectively recalled, to a purpose. The accounts, of course, differed across the different lives of my participants, but found their meaning within a cultural paradigm—of devotion itself as bhakti, its emotional correlate as a relationship—but also of concepts such as "intuitive insight," (anubhuti), the *man*, and smrti, both remembrance and recollection, where this relationship between human and divine transcended "meaning" and became meaningful and thus, transformational.

The narratives I present in the next section are of two main types: (a) dreams (*svapna,* sometimes as "dream-instruction" *svapnades*, or precognitive, as predictive of future events); and (b) *alaukik ghatana*, "miraculous events," which could include dreams, waking visions, or the surprising, apparently inexplicable actions of humans who could be the deity herself manifest. Dreams are immediate, unmediated, "veridical" experience (see also Pechilis 2012, 131). Precognitive dreams depended, I was given to understand, explicitly or implicitly on the spiritual merit of the "seer," merit possibly acquired over lifetimes. Such merit may be an inherent quality of a devotee as unrealized potential, or acquired through meditation and austerities which strengthen the *man*.[11] Other experiences may also be related to a person's proximity to other and meritorious devotees—simply being in the vicinity of such a person. A "miraculous event" could involve rectifying a ritual lapse, by drawing in a stranger to do the needful. Often, such experiences whether as dreams, dream-related events, and events themselves were attributed to the *krpa* ("compassion") of the goddess, a gift, analogous to "auspicious sight" (darsan) granted by her to the meritorious devotee.[12]

The second category, miraculous intervention by Kali (or guru), can be in a life crisis, such as illness in the family, where Kali's maternal compassion (as Sakti, channeled through the powers of her conduit, the guru) resolves the crisis. This is seen as extraordinary again because it is inexplicable by everyday logic. While dreams are unsolicited, succor in a life crisis may be solicited by the devotee in a heartfelt prayer to the goddess or in an act of ritual, most powerfully efficacious as animal sacrifice, "gift" (balidan), or as blood-offering from the body of the devotee, as "self-offering," (*atmabali*). Narratives of experiences related to blood offerings to Kali were distinct from others I would hear, however. Especially where an offering "failed" stories spoke of dire consequences for the devotee, even his family. The moral caliber of the person making the offering, even with the best of intentions, was directly related to any calamity that followed—but could not be proven, as such caliber could be related to infractions in a previous life as well as in this one.

Whether as dreams, visions, or events, experiences related to Kali/Sakti, albeit recounted in narrative, are ultimately ineffable, inexplicable by ordinary logic. Everyday boundaries between sleeping and waking, between deity and human, even between deity and animal are fluid, flowing, and merged, like Sakti itself. As far as this is possible, the "interpretation" of dreams and events lies generally in a concurrence of a particular point in time and space for the worshiper, resulting in some definite, observable, and undeniable resolution or prediction fulfilled—as "real"—and interpreted as compassionate and powerful divine intervention. Precognitive dreams, likewise, are validated in their fruition. As events over a life, such experiences as insights into the workings of Sakti, add dimension to one's sense of being a part of that larger Self, Sakti writ large, and provide a tentative insight into the essential question which Alokebabu asked rhetorically: "Who am 'I'?" Such permeable "boundaries" were evidently possible, a way of existing in the world, one which, in Kripal's words, does not deny the "impossible," allowing for "miraculous" experiences even among non-mystics, the "ordinary" people who shared their stories with me. As anubhuti, variously, such experiences and how they are interpreted offer tentative answers to that question, the "I" or self, the atman, on a journey that is transformative of that self.

NOTES

1. Murray, in a review of writers on narrative, notes the many forms narratives can take, as also the many forms of interviews (as the source of the narratives). Narratives can be extended to written forms of experience (diaries, letters), as also documentary forms, like autobiographies and archival sources, and also visual narratives (2018, 264).

2. Murray notes that storytelling is "endemic in qualitative interviews," and that the unstructured interview can foster storytelling (2018, 266). He further notes the reflexivity required on the part of the interviewer (269), and the empathy [he] needs to demonstrate (268). It is in the free-flowing conversation with participants about their lives and particular experiences within which smaller (and larger) stories emerge (268).

3. In the Indian context McDaniel (1989) describes ecstatic states among Bengali mystics, locating these within the Bhakti tradition. Babb (1986) explains the validity

of the extranormal in urban Hindu sects within the hierarchical transactions of caste relations, in this context between preceptor and disciple.

4. See David Presti, on attempts by neuroscientists and psychiatrists to scientifically establish, by controlled experiment, the validity of the paranormal—but acknowledging the difficulty of doing so with "spontaneous" experiences (2018).

5. Murray notes the weakening of an interest in narrative data in the social sciences with the "rise of positivism" and the association of such data with the arts and humanities (2018, 281). See also Matilal (1977, 4) in Chapter 2, earlier, who makes the point, like Obeyesekere, that acknowledging the mystical did not preclude logical argument by Indian philosophical schools.

6. In Hindi and Bengali (both northern Indian languages), *alaukik* suggests the "other worldly." See also Gold, whose Rajasthani worshipers describe the miracle as *chamatkari ghatana*, "wondrous event" (in Dempsey & Raj 2008).

7. Recall my radiologist father's description of his dreams of Kali, and his interpretation in the Introduction, and matter-of-fact attitude to these experiences.

8. Harman (in Raj & Dempsey 2008) notes that a miracle is an experience rather than an event, even though it refers to one in the observable world. But miracle as experience is an interpretation of an event (or a symbol or sign, as Kripal also notes, 2010). Raj, in the same volume, notes that "tangible experience" explains the "tenacity of the miraculous" (2008). The "miracle" then also lies in interpreting what is being communicated in the "experience," thereby giving it substance and reality. However, Rinehart (in Raj & Dempsey, op. cit.) writes on Swami Vivekananda, Ramakrishna's disciple, positing the rigor and practice that underlies the apparent "miracles" of the yogi, or of "miracles" associated with Ramakrishna himself, to counter, as he travels to the West in the late nineteenth century, charges against the "superstitions" imputed to Hindu beliefs.

9. In his study of the Christian meaning of grace in a Swedish church Stromberg observes that believers "seize" cultural meanings, "discovered . . . in emotional moments of profound insight . . . These moments of discovery are apt to be labeled by believers as experiences of grace . . . [where] the symbol blends with experiences . . . . It is a relation of meaningfulness, not only of meaning" (1986, 12–13).

10. See Kripal on the "narrative construction" by devotees through selective interpretive memory (smrti) of dreams and visions of her, in the hagiographic tradition, of Ramakrishna's wife, Sharada Devi, where she herself is "silent" (2001, 172–173).

11. According to Potter (1977), the Nyaya-Vaisesika school of thought held that dreams may be due to "destiny" or "fate" *adrsta* (literally, "unseen"). If they presage good to come, this may be related to the merit (*dharma*) of the dreamer.

12. Babb (1981) and Eck (1981) describe the ritual act of darsan where the worshiper "looks" upon the image of the deity, and is "seen" by her, in a transactional act of "visual consummation" (Babb 1981, 391). It is a state of heightened perception in the act, and in the experience, a "seeing" more extraordinary and potentially transformational for the devotee. My participants also described dreams as darsan.

Part II

NARRATIVES OF EXPERIENCE

Chapter 4

The Guru as Conduit for Kali/ Sakti, Disciples' Experiences

A devotee's bhakti, both love and faith, establishes a relationship with a human of high spiritual stature, the guru, who is seen as Kali/Sakti's conduit. This chapter frames and offers context to the narratives of devotees and disciples to follow, as well as to the next two chapters—on a guru himself, Alokebabu (chapter 5), and Bani's story of her "journey" to "receiving" or "realizing" her mother Kali, facilitated by several gurus, including Alokebabu (chapter 6). The persona of the guru, however, plays a role in chapters to follow, even if not centrally.

The text *Srisrigurugita* interprets the two syllables, "*gu*" and "*ru*" respectively as "darkness/ignorance," *avidya*, and "awakening" or "light," as "truth," satya. Such "darkness" is also the embodied being's inability to see beyond his or her limited life and its attachments to it, which a guru of genuine spiritual caliber is able to reveal to the dedicated, persevering aspirant/disciple.[1] The preface and following commentary that precedes the *Srisrigurugita* itself in Raghubarananda (1987) observes that (I paraphrase and translate from Bengali) "there is no difference between a human and the sakti that moves him. It is Sakti as eternal "force" or "energy" that finds bodily form in a human, and it is the person who gives that Sakti shape. However Sakti can and does exist without shape, and beyond the person. This Sakti can be transferred (or "travel") from one person to another. The human who cannot see beyond his individual existence (who is blinded by or bounded by "illusion") is awakened and enlightened by one who can do so. Such a person is the guru, who embodies guru-sakti."[2]

As described in scripture, then, the guru is both human, but also the "eternal" guru. When he dies, his sakti is not lost, and he continues, in his compassion to see to his disciples' well-being. Such powers are not obtained by book learning or punditry, say the commentators on the *Srisrigurugita* (and included in this edited text, 1987), but there as inherent potential and also acquired by such persons. Those who pursue the path of the guru do so not from greed or for material acquisition. The guru does not boast of his powers, but rather, conceals them. He lives in, but is not of the world, a renunciant in spirit and in person. Ultimately, the true guru, who is teacher, mentor, and father-figure, is able to direct, and possibly reveal to the disciple his own true and divine, but heretofore unseen self, atman.

The persona of the guru himself, and relationship with the disciple has drawn considerable interest among Western scholars and I discuss both indigenous and other perspectives before I present my participants' accounts later in this chapter. Scholars have brought cultural, social and psychological perspectives on interpretations of the guru-disciple relationship. Kakar, a psychoanalyst, notes the indigenous emphasis on the psychic abilities of gurus and healers, and suggests that their powers are effective because the "patient" believes in the reality of such powers (1982). Babb sees the asymmetric relationship of guru and disciple as meaningful because they reflect caste hierarchy (1986). Vail (1985) and Babb (op. cit.) both note the centrality of the concept of Sakti as a divine "current" which is fluid, and invisibly permeates the material world. It is less focused among those who are not spiritually advanced but radiant and concentrated in holy and awakened persons such as gurus. Such power may be dispensed and communicated by the guru as an act of the will to the deserving disciple.

Mlecko[3] observes that the guru means many things, and is an entity who has no counterpart in Western culture: "For the guru is a teacher, counselor, father-image . . . hero, source of strength, even divinity integrated into one personality" (1982, 34). While being "fully human" the guru is divinity, and a vehicle for divine grace. Today, the guru may flout caste distinctions and serve as an exemplar for "exercising free choice . . . [and] deal with matters spiritual, political or even occupational" (58). The guru, across different sectarian beliefs, is a spiritual guide, and is qualified to impart such knowledge to a disciple primarily because he possesses experiential knowledge, beyond the texts, of "ultimate values . . . within the Hindu tradition" (34). In the Tantric tradition, the guru has "extraordinary power" (46). In the Bhakti tradition, he is revered, again, less for knowledge of texts and scriptures but rather for his personal realization of the divine (46). Kabir (1440–1518?), a renowned saint who was influenced by both Sufi Islam and Bhakti Hindu beliefs, described the guru as someone who could carry humans across "the obstacle-laden river of life" (in Mlecko 1982, 48). Swami Sivananda (1887–1962), Mlecko notes, was a medical doctor turned renunciant, who gave up his book learning, career and wealth (see Ananda's story for a contemporary account, in chapter 7). The spiritual stature of the guru is achieved, rather, through direct knowledge of the divine through "*anubhava,*" "experience" (54).

Copeman and Ikegame, in an edited volume (2012) take studies of the South Asian guru further, and offer interdisciplinary perspectives from the viewpoint of diverse "social engagements," such as the significance of female gurus, gurus in Islam, and in the context of economic liberalization in contemporary India. In the introduction the editors describe the guru as having crossed several domains. However, the guru "is not reducible to any of them . . . we suggest that the multiplicity and diversity of these interventions points towards a sense of the guru's *uncontainability*" (2012, 3). The editors attribute this to the polyvalent meanings of gurus (3; see also Mlecko 1982). In this volume, Gold comments on continuities in the face of change, where gurus and their successors continue to offer "a specific mantra, enlightening, teaching, and/or spiritual power" as the means of salvation for devotees (2012, 241).

I would hear prolific accounts of experiences from participants as related to gurus, interspersed with their observations on how they understood the powers of such persons, reflecting those in the *Srisrigurugita* and in scholarship. Gurus are both perceived and described as conduits for Kali's divine Sakti—a "force" which is embodied in the guru's human person but is also present as a force which cannot be depleted in the "eternal" guru. Once established, such a relationship not only persists through life, but even after his death, as a guru can be asked for advice, or reborn into a disciple's family. The saint Ramakrishna, can draw, in a dream, a sceptic to a devotee's home temple, while a bright light awakens a newly initiated disciple, and is described as his guru's sakti, given to him as a gift (denoting by implication the disciple's own spiritual potential). Alokebabu, while denying his powers strenuously to me is seen (and believed) by Bani to heal an ailing guru across vast distances (powers ascribed to gurus in accounts by other participants as well). Some devotees/disciples would recount ritual instructions by dream from their guru, while others spoke of remarkable incidents related to their gurus witnessed in person, such as Chandu's story, to follow.

While I would find my participants' gurus variously affiliated with the Vaisnava, Saiva, or Sakta/Tantric traditions, the relationship between preceptor and disciple was clearly an asymmetric one, where the disciple/devotee sought spiritual guidance (and often, succor and support in life's travails) from his or her guru. I would not find this relationship expressly stated in terms of caste differences, except, as we will see in Sachin's story, as transcendence of such differences; or, as we shall see later, in a devotee, Ananda (a Brahman himself), calling into question Alokebabu, also a Brahman, about a ritual act when in a state of pollution (in this case a hand unwashed after eating). The themes which Mlecko traces across traditions find consistent refrains in my participants' own comments on the powers of their gurus. They described him as deity made manifest—generally the god Siva, but

also Kali (more accurately Kali as Sakti), thus embodying the qualities of
divinity as one, transcendent of gender. The guru's own human mentors, in a
spiritual genealogy, were perceived to be, like him, Siva reborn. Participants
emphasized the guru's direct and experiential realization of divinity as
taking precedence over his knowledge of sacred texts. Ramakrishna, an
illiterate man, instructed by emphasis on experiencing divinity rather than
accumulating knowledge (Mlecko op. cit., 52). Ananda validates his own
experiences with those of Ramakrishna's, while meditating, referring to the
latter's words as recorded in the *Kathamrta*. Accounts also imply, however,
that this quality, while possibly inherent in such persons, is developed over
time through disciplined practice, making the guru especially perceptive of
such potential, in turn, in those who seek his (or her) guidance. The aspirant, on his or her part, also must persevere with dedication to perceive this
quality in a guru, and be selective.[4] Because of his own sakti the guru is
able to "open" his disciples' eyes, and communicate that power. Conveyed
by means of a "seed-sound," *bijamantra*, particular to each deity, the guru
realizes the particular "frequency" of that sound in a person, whispers the
sound into his or her ear, and sets up a connection between his disciple and
a particular divinity.[5] Alokebabu explained to me: "The guru understands.
Like a doctor seeing a patient and realizing what ails him, the real guru
realizes the sound." Kali's devotees interpreted their relationship with, and
experiences of their gurus—as a conduit of divine power—in story. Dinu,
Bani's husband, observed:

> The sakti of the guru and the Sakti of the Mother Kali are the same. This Sakti
> is both inside and outside our bodies. The guru's sakti is really the eternal Sakti
> of the eternal guru of which he is an embodiment. He is a medium, and we need
> his sakti to awaken us. He is director and executive. He puts kohl[6] on our eyes,
> making us see clearly. He shows us the way, he gives us a push in the right
> direction.

The guru reciprocates with compassion that which his disciple offers,
devotion, bhakti, with pure *man*. The guru's own anubhuti, his intuitive
knowledge of divine mystery enables him to have precognitive awareness
of a crisis (a distant disciple's ill health), and its possible resolution. He is
capable of directing his sakti to alleviate the crisis, in an act of compassion,
and by willed intent. Asit, a male devotee, observed that his experiences in
relation to his guru have solved many problems in his life, and brought him
peace of mind: "My experiences [related to his guru] have drawn me close
to the Mother Kali."

The following account by Bani and Dinu's son, Chandu, 30, illustrates
some of the perceived powers of the guru:

I used to go around even when I was very young with our gurudev[7]. . . . I had learned in school that Jesus had parted the ocean [Chandu confuses Jesus with Moses]. I went once with gurudev to Tarakesvar [a holy site near Kolkata]. There is a lake there, from where water is used to bathe Siva.[8] I watched gurudev bathe there, in *padmasan* [sitting cross-legged, in the "lotus position" in yoga]. He was floating on the water, with his hands on his chest.

"How did you understand this?" I asked. Chandu replied:

I wondered how this was possible? I am a good swimmer, and my father was a participant in the Asian games in water polo. But when gurudev floated towards the shore [still sitting upright], I have nothing to say. When he left his padmasan, he sank into the water. These little incidents created in me the sense of something beyond what we can explain rationally.

As with ritual worship of the iconic deity, the relationship between guru and disciple involves, for example, the ritual offering of food to the guru by disciples, and its return to and consumption by the disciple as the guru's "grace" (prasad)—food now imbued with the guru's sakti. The guru's touch in blessing conveys his sakti to the disciple, as does darsan, a "visual exchange" between guru and disciple, or merely the act of looking on his (sometimes her) person. Hearing the guru speak on religious matters also fills the disciple with sakti (so, a female participant, Manju, would invite holy men to speak at her organization Mangolik's weekly hymn-singing events). Sakti, as a communicable power effects a transformation in substances (such as food or flowers), in the *man*, and therefore in the person or "self" of the receptive disciple.

Chandu believed that their guru remains with the family, even after his death [in 1980]: "After gurudev's death I have seen him in dreams many times. . . . I have faith in him. If I talk with him . . . I get results. I believe this, I won't return empty-handed . . . just because of his spiritual achievements." Their guru could see into his (Chandu's) previous life, one where, the guru claimed, he, (Chandu), had renounced family life and become a renunciant. "So," Chandu said to me, "In this life I spend more time with my family." Other participants would speak of the abilities of gurus, including Alokebabu, to not only be able to see the past lives of others, but also their own.

However, while different persons may manifest their powers to potential disciples, not all such experiences lead to the establishing of a connection between guru and disciple, even though these might "disturb the *man*." This can be a pragmatic issue (one cannot afford the gifts required to be given to a guru at initiation), or simply a feeling that a particular guru is not appropriate for the aspiring disciple. However, once accepted as such, and established by means of "initiation" (*diksa*), the relationship between guru and disciple develops and generally becomes increasingly close over the course of time. The guru, called variously Baba ("father") or Dada ("older brother"),[9] not only teaches his disciples about spiritual advancement and ritual, but also, as with Alokebabu, serves as a benevolent and parental figure, guiding, advising, admonishing, or scolding, as occasion requires.

The accounts to follow emphasize, sometimes explicitly, but mostly implicitly in their emotional manner of narration, how such experiences move the disciple/devotee to affirmation of his or her spiritual potential, but also, implicitly or explicitly, to spiritual transformation. The fortuitous and ultimately inexplicable nature of these experiences and their lack of conclusive closure find meaning in the mystery that is Kali/Sakti herself. The accounts I heard from participants, as related to their gurus, fell broadly into three contexts: an aspirant's quest for a guru, finding the appropriate person, and experiences following initiation by the guru; the guru's miraculous healing powers; and connections with the guru after his death, as a child reborn in the disciple/devotee's family. These narratives, like others I will present in later chapters, take different shapes and structures: some are longer and chronological, others shorter, more illustrative of a point the narrator wishes to make about the guru's powers. However, each account incorporates the narrator's own reflections and commentary, offering his or her own interpretation of the guru-disciple relationship, and again, explicitly or implicitly suggesting his or her transformation in this relationship. The various accounts simultaneously make reference to prevailing beliefs about the entity, beyond merely human, which is the guru. In Kripal's observation, he is invested with qualities, or "constructed" by disciples' experiences of his powers even as the disciple is "constructed" within this relationship (2001).[10]

ACCOUNTS RELATED TO INITIATION (*DIKSA*)

Alokebabu, with his customary bluntness, observed that when he gave the diksa mantra to an initiate he "said clearly" that he was not selling his services for money, flowers, or even salutation: "I am not that kind of guru." He gave the "sound incantation" to a disciple simply so he could call on that particular deity. His own relationship with his disciple involved wishing the latter "well-being," mangal, tersely again noting, "This is not a business." He also noted that most people came to his temple with problems, which they did not admit until they were about to leave two hours later. If they needed something from him, they should have said so: "They are lying to the giver of the mantra" [here, himself, the guru]. His words explained the wooden board on his temple wall forbidding even salutations to the guru!

The guru, with his powers, perceives in a disciple's *man* a frequency or "seed-sound" particular to a deity. This "seed" is "unuttered," *abyakta*, and is tuned to the eternal and divine, primal sound, *Om*. When uttered, this seed-sound combines with other sounds to take form as the monosyllabic "seed-incantation." The ritual mental repetition, *japa*, of the incantation focuses the *man*, destroys egotism (which blinds to seeing the truth), and accumulates sakti in the disciple. Once the guru has intuited, as anubhuti, a disciple's particular predilection for a deity, he initiates the latter by whispering the incantation three times into his or her ear. Participants described this act as "sowing a seed into the right environment." Their *man*, they said, changes after initiation, and for some, the experiences that followed confirmed this new path.

Although the seed-incantations for different deities are openly known, once the mantra is imparted by the guru to the disciple it is not to be revealed or uttered to anyone (including the ethnographer). It is the special and individual mantra by which the disciple is tuned to divine power, his or her unique connection with the eternal Sakti. Such a mantra not only calls on the deity, but also implores her protection. Thus, Kali's seed-incantation is *krim*, which translates, in terms of its individual sound components, as "Great Illusion, Mother of the Universe, remove my sorrow" (*Srisri Kalipuja Paddhati*).

The transmission of the seed-incantation in the rite of diksa has momentous effects on the newly initiated, giving impetus to a relationship with the guru that approximates the closeness of a biological relationship. This impetus is related, as I was implicitly given to understand, to the disciple's realization that the guru had observed a special spiritual potential in him or her. A woman described how the senior monk at the Ramakrishna Mission had picked her out of a crowd, even at age 16, and asked her to take diksa. A male participant described his own experience after diksa:

> I've had many anubhuti. . . . One such experience was when after initiation, whenever I looked at my guru's photograph, I could see the faces of the Mother Kali and Ramakrishna merging with it. It wasn't a dream, or an optical illusion. I saw this with my third eye [he touched the center of his forehead]. I saw this vision over some four months. Then I told my guru about my experience, and never saw it again. Maybe he took it away from me.

SACHIN

Sachin narrated a story about how he found his guru, the man who would initiate him. The search is integral to his story, revealing of both the guru's powers, and implicitly of Sachin's own potential. His story tells of apparent connections between two holy men, the first of whom he met on a plane journey, the second while he was on a bus in Kolkata. That both gurus see Sachin's spiritual potential is implied in the telling, the first possibly wanting to offer him diksa on the plane itself. Both gurus are protective of him. The first seems to express concern whether Sachin is being met at the airport after the plane lands; the second sits next to him on a bus with only two remaining empty seats, and purchases a bus ticket for him. The two even look like each other, wonderful in appearance, like the god Siva himself as Sachin tells me. Sachin then describes his experience after his diksa, and ultimately, how he is changed.

I first met Sachin's wife Sumona washing the stairs leading to the sanctum at Kalighat Temple, as an act of merit for her ailing husband. She invited me to their home where she, Sachin, and their then-nineteen-year old son Mukul lived. I would meet a slight man of over sixty years at the time. Sachin had worked as a draftsman in a tea firm, and was now retired. The oldest of seven brothers and four sisters, Sachin had lost his mother when he was young and had been brought up by his maternal aunts. His share of the house, jointly owned by him and his brothers, was a dark, small room on the ground floor, with access to the common kitchen and bathroom at the rear of the house. The musty little room with one large bed, a meat safe (for nonrefrigerated storage of food), and a wooden rack piled high with clothes were witness to the hardship in which this family lived. A small altar, built into the wall, had framed prints of Kali and a stone Sivalingam.

I began, as I usually did, with the question, how do you understand the Mother Kali? This question inspired an outpouring of stories, ranging from accounts of inexplicable moving lights that insistently led Sachin to discover sacred stones that represented, in his view, Kali; and of dreams, validated by holy men and gurus, enabling him to discover hidden in an uprooted tree branch a figure of the elephant god Ganesa. Both Sumona and Mukul would tell me when I met them again in my second phase of research that Sachin had a "quality apart, much above their own" who "received a lot through dreams." In that first conversation with me, Sachin, who had "always" been drawn to the spiritual life, said quietly and simply:

"I especially like Kali. We've always worshipped her in this household. Everyone told me that I would find my Mother so close one day."

At that earlier meeting Sumona mentioned how difficult their search for a guru had been, and the many that they had met but not been happy with. She had gone with Sachin's advice: "He asked me not to fret. He said that our guru would come to us. He was right." I present Sachin's narrative below, describing the apparently serendipitous events which led to his ultimately meeting with the man who would become his guru:

In 1966 I took a flight to North Bengal on work and met a sadhu [holy man] on the plane. He seemed to be an important person, and the air-hostess asked me to move to another seat so the sadhu could have both seats on which to lie down. Of course I did so. After a while we flew into a bad storm. I looked at the sadhu and was amazed to see a bright orange glow around him. I asked the passenger next to me if he too saw the glow around the sadhu.

The passenger said, "It's probably a reflection from the red saris of the women on the plane."

Sachin observed to me, "This simply wasn't so." He continued:

The glow was so wonderful I cannot describe it in words—so powerful—a light the color of an orange. And then the sadhu called me to him.

I went over, and touched his feet in salutation. He gave me his blessing by touching my head. I might have received my diksa there on the plane, but somehow I felt this wasn't my guru, so I let it go. When we reached our destination I had to wait as I was going to be met. While I waited, a crowd of people with garlands came up to greet the holy man. But he seemed to be waiting too, and was looking at me. One of his followers told me, "He's waiting to see if you are being met, if you're in trouble." I replied that I was alright. After this experience I was somehow disturbed, my *man* felt as if something was pulling at it.

Then, shortly after Sachin returned to Kolkata, while on a crowded bus going to work with only two empty seats remaining, a sadhu who looked very much like the man he had met on the plane came over and sat next to him: "He was wonderful of appearance, with matted hair just like Siva. I wanted to touch his feet, but felt shy to do so."

The sadhu asked Sachin where he was going, and then bought two tickets (to central Kolkata). Sachin kept his ticket: "I have it to this day."

The sadhu asked him if he was married, and Sachin mentioned his family. The holy man then asked if Sachin had taken diksa, to which Sachin replied that he had not, and asked if he could recommend a guru. At this point the sadhu asked if Sachin would take diksa from him. Sachin described this conversation on the bus:

I didn't know if this man was genuine, or whether he was conning me. So I said, 'There's a strike on at my firm and I can't afford diksa at present.' The sadhu replied that I would need only a *haritaki* [myrobalam] fruit and a sacred thread, and to come to the asram the next morning at 9 a.m., after bathing.

Sachin did not tell me of the details of his initiation other than that he was "very excited and full of sakti," and arrived at the guru's place two hours earlier, at 7 a.m. Sachin then described his experience after his initiation:

Now, I'm sharing this with you. I was so happy after my diksa, I was lying in bed repeating my bijamantra. My wife and son were asleep. Suddenly I saw a light through the window—this was around 4 a.m. It was brighter than the sun, and lit up the whole room. The light entered the room and struck me on the right shoulder. I screamed. Everybody woke up asking, "What's happening?" Remember, I was quite awake when it happened. My *man* was very disturbed by this experience, and, as soon as it was light, I bathed and ran to my gurudev's asram. My guru-ma [the guru's wife] was there. She said, "You've received it so soon? This is not easy to receive. So your guru has given you sakti!"

I asked Sachin how his guru explained the strange light.
Sachin answered briefly but eloquently:

It was she, Sakti herself, who manifests herself as light. My gurudev said that such anubhuti happen on the path of spiritual discipline. The guru is my father, and he is also all the gods, Brahma, Visnu, Siva." Sachin added, "My guru is especially close to me, and loves me dearly—he has stayed more than a month in my house.

Sachin, as we talked over tea, then told me of other experiences following his initiation.

I used to be afraid to do the rituals for Kali at home despite my gurudev's instructions and reassurances. This goddess can be dangerous and demanding. But he said to me, "Sit on your prayer mat and remember me in your *man* before starting your worship, and I will protect you." Since then, whatever I have wanted in my *man* I have received. Two years afterward, I received my gurudev's sakti again. He gave me the mantra for the *homa* [fire] ritual[11] in a dream. I also didn't know how to worship Krsna and Radha. I dreamed that my guru was standing in the middle of three streets giving me ritual instructions. I awoke and wrote these down immediately. The next day I went to see him, and he said "You've received the primal mantra, 'Om.' You'll receive plenty; go cautiously, don't waste anything."

Sachin illustrated how sakti in a disciple might be lost if initiated by the wrong guru with this account:

I met a woman Tantric who called me "a high-class student" and wanted to initiate me, in exchange for some food which I was to give to her [as part of the rite]. After being warned by my gurudev that I might lose sakti, I refused diksa from the Tantric though I did offer her food. I now pray mostly at home. I hardly ever go even to Kalighat Temple. But I do go to my gurudev for advice, and I live by his blessings.

Sachin concluded with an event related to his guru, as credentials for the man's powers to prove, he said, "who [his guru] *really* was":[12]

My gurudev used to study forensic medicine in a medical school in Kolkata. But he gave it all up to be a Tantric, performing rites to Kali at the cremation grounds. If you meet my guru he'll attract you. While he was studying medicine, a certain event inspired him. One day, coming out of medical college, he saw a man dressed in saffron[13] picking food out of a heap of bloodied garbage. "That fellow must be mad," thought my gurudev, and then he saw the man was actually a friend of his. He scolded him, saying he [his friend] would fall sick. The friend asked for a cigarette. As their hands touched, my gurudev felt an electric current pass through him. Then his friend asked to be dropped off at his home in North Kolkata, saying, "I'm your friend, I'm giving you something. While I'm alive you won't realize the significance of what it is. Only when I'm gone." Then he gave my gurudev a Visnu *salagrama* [the god Visnu in the form of a black ovoid stone] in a bag. He told my gurudev that he [my guru] would one day renounce worldly life. When my gurudev's friend died there was a tremendous storm, you couldn't see three feet ahead. And his prediction about my gurudev came true.

When I ask how his devotional life differed from that of his wife, Sachin observed that while the bijamantra may be the same for both (he did not know her mantra), their rituals were different, and that this was an individual choice—"the Mother [Kali] makes us do things." Where others went by the book, he did not. His guru's wife advised him to follow his *man*. Sumona, he said, followed the path of her maternal grandmother; he didn't know and did not ask. He quoted Ramakrishna, that there are as many paths as there are beliefs. However, his prayer rituals did have some structure, albeit non-traditional. Instead of beginning with prayers to Ganesa, then Siva, he began with prayers to his guru, followed by prayers to Siva, ending with Kali, his "chosen" deity (*istadevata*). Sachin concluded with the changes in himself after having been with his guru over some time:

I learned to overcome caste distinctions after I met my guru. He was a Brahman, but used to eat food and drink coconut milk with his non-Brahman disciples [including himself, of the second-tier Kayastha caste]. He [the guru] was not concerned with being polluted by doing this. We disciples are like sons and daughters to him. And so I eat off the same plate that is used by the servants in our house. I became more flexible about ritual, using tap water instead of sacred Ganga water for worship.

If his *man* was pure, Sachin observed, then he could say his prayers even in the toilet without risk of spiritual pollution, and that he now had a more comfortable, less fearful relationship with Kali:

If I call upon the Mother Kali in a crisis, she hears me always. Whatever I truly desire in my *man* or need desperately, such as money, I receive this. I too can now protect other people. I say a special mantra for someone wanting to know, for example, if a project is going to succeed, and I place a flower on top of the Sivalingam when I'm praying. If the flower falls off Siva the project will be successful. I've done this for you.

I asked, "Did the flower fall?"

Sachin replied that it did, and gave me the flower to keep. After instructions received in a dream, he continued, he would give out wooden beads from sacred garlands to protect people against a heart attack. This worked with an ailing neighbor, who, in return, regularly sent him flowers for his daily worship, which Sachin would have found too expensive to purchase.

Sachin's story does not end here. I will return to his home five years later, in my second phase of fieldwork, and share more in the Afterword to this book.

EXPERIENCES OF THE GURU'S HEALING POWERS

The guru, once a relationship is formalized through diksa, sustains the disciple by being "inner-dwelling," *antaryami*, in Dinu's words, revealing that he knows the inner wants, fears, and feelings of his disciple. This is seen as evidence of his love and compassion, experienced through, for example, his miraculous powers of healing. This too is Sakti at work, working through the guru's touch, or his verbal assurance, and/or also through certain rituals, such as that of sacrifice as "self-offering" (atmabali), where blood from the guru's own chest or right arm is offered to the goddess into sacred fire, homa.

Chandu had the following account of his experiences to share, prefaced by his early and uncertain bhakti.

He was attending a Catholic school in southwest Kolkata, and staying in the school's hostel. While he felt, (given his spiritually minded parents, Dinu and Bani), there were "fruits" to be gained from worship, his own devotion was, perhaps, "not what it should be." But, he said, he felt that that "someone is there," to whom he could express his sorrows. Then he would meet the man who would become their family's guru, and who would inspire him to devotion:

> I was then in Class 6 or 7, we were living in this house, and our gurudev was staying with us [on a visit]. A message came for him, saying a disciple of his had severe hepatitis, and wanted to see him. Our guru was shocked and quiet. In the evening he said to me, once you have finished your studies you and I will

go out together. We went first to Keoratala cremation grounds. There he prayed, sitting there, while I held his clothes, for 30–45 minutes.

He lit a lot of incense sticks. See, I was very young, and knew little of what was going on, so I [saw it as worship]. He was naked except for a loincloth. After he was done . . . he picked up three lit sticks from his worship and threw them on the water. He said, "I'm throwing these on the water, if they stay alight my disciple will live. If they don't, he will die."

You may not believe me, I was so young . . . but what I saw remains with me today. Three incense sticks flowed away along the current, and as far as I could see, the sticks remained alight, in a river that was full. You can call this magic [*sic*], or you can call it spiritual. The disciple lived.

Dinu recounted another story to illustrate the guru's powers of intuition, and of healing. Once, when their guru was staying with them, he heard him suddenly exclaim in the middle of the night when everyone was asleep:

I was irritated, and called out, "What's the matter?"

My gurudev said, "My disciple Gaur's son is very ill! Go and open the door of the worship room."

I did so, and my gurudev went in to the altar room. He seemed to know beforehand where all the items of worship were kept. He lit three sticks of incense and began to pray.

After a little he said, "The boy's better now. Get me some tea."

By now it was 4:45 a.m., said Dinu. His guru then asked Bani for some food to take with them, and, with Dinu, took a taxi to Gaur's house in North Calcutta. Gaur was sleeping exhaustedly, having been up all night with his sick child. His parents were weeping for their eldest grandchild. The guru advised a change of doctors, which was done. Within five days the boy recovered fully. After the child was well, the guru asked Gaur to offer worship at the asram on the night of the new moon [especially auspicious to Kali], and to take a cotton towel, fruit, flowers, and clarified butter as offerings. He then gave Gaur the consecrated flowers, saying to him, "Put these in an amulet, and put the amulet on your son. It will protect him."

Dinu concluded: "The child is now about twelve years old."

It is noteworthy, however, that Dinu's guru did not exclude modern medicine in his advice to his disciple, which I would see with Alokebabu's advice in such situations as well. Dinu described the death of his guru, and its cause, one of healing a disciple, in an act of compassion and protection:

The guru has the ability to absorb into himself the suffering of his disciple, even though he himself might lose years off his life. In fact, that is how my gurudev met his early death. When a disciple of our guru, a man who was the only heir to his family, became sick with a brain tumor, our gurudev "took on the weight" [*bhar nilen*] of the tumor. Not long after he marked the calendar for a certain day and time, and he "left his body" [*deha rakhlen*] that day.

But as we will see in the account to follow, this time by Babul, Chandu's wife, the guru's death does not sever his connection with beloved disciples.

POSTHUMOUS CONNECTIONS WITH THE GURU

Even after his death the guru continues to be a vital presence in the lives of some of his disciples, as Chandu observed. Posthumous experiences of his sakti as love and protection maintain this connection, which, according to disciples, is possible only because of the guru's spiritual caliber and compassion, and again, an act that is willed by him.

Dinu's guru had been born in Nirjharesvar Temple (the Siva temple within the precincts of the Kali temple at Daksinesvar, near Kolkata). Dinu told me how, when his guru lay dying, he had said, "After I am gone, come to Nirjharesvar Temple in times of need and speak to me." He wept copiously as he recalled his guru's death. He and his family had been going to Nirjharesvar Temple ever since.

Dinu continued:

My gurudev may not be physically with me ever since his death [in 1980], but we're not really separated. When I call him he hears me . . . he's given me a guide rope. I'm no holy man with special powers, only a householder with a lot of baggage. When I need guidance I pray to his picture, and if he doesn't respond I pray till he does. If he approves I know he'll smile at me. If his face looks sullen, round as a rice-pot, then I won't proceed.

Before I spoke with you I prayed to my gurudev to give me sakti to say the right words. He smiled, so I am speaking with you! I also confess to my guru when I do anything wrong, and ask for his forgiveness.

Dinu's daughter-in-law Babul, who, with her in-laws was convinced that their deceased guru has been reborn as her older child, a boy of about four at the first time I met the family, offered the following account:

I always suffer as a consequence of the bad things I do. If I get angry with anyone my day is full of ups and downs which I can't explain. I feel too that my children were born under remarkable circumstances, after special vows made to our guru, and to my grandmother-in-law.

I love children, but, at first I couldn't conceive. Everyone advised me not to worry about it, but I became emotional and worried, thinking something was wrong with me. So Didi, [she addressed me as "older sister"], when we find no other way out, God [she uses the generic word bhagaban] is our only answer. I've often had visions when praying at the home altar, and I've also had many dreams [of guru and deity]. But I had no idea what was about to happen.

With this preamble, she continued:

In October I went to Daksinesvar to visit the Nirjharesvar temple. I believe that Siva is reborn again and again, and that our guru was Siva himself. He had arranged my marriage, but died before the ceremony. He had done so much for us, but couldn't be there [for the wedding]. I wanted him to come close to me, as my son, I prayed for this with bhakti in my *man*. So I went to the Siva temple at Nirjharesvar. Though I didn't do much by way of ritual, I called upon our gurudev with all my *man* to come to me as my son. I vowed that if I had a child I would come and offer worship at this temple.

As I was coming out of the temple, I saw a kitten sitting by the door—a little kitten, white as milk, as if it had just been born. The twelve Siva temples stand in a row at Dakkhinevar, if you go to one, you must go to offer worship at all of them. I saw the kitten as I left to go to the next temple, but didn't think anything of it. But the cat followed me, mewing. As I prayed at the other temples, the kitten stayed outside like a guard, just sitting there. As I left that temple it followed me again, mewing, to each and every temple. After my worship was done I made my way down the steep stairs [from the temple]. It couldn't follow me, it was so small. So it stood at the top of the stairs and mewed loudly. There were a lot of people about, but it followed only me. Now, I hadn't seen the kitten when I first entered the temple. Only after I had prayed did I see it! I was irritated by its constant mewing. My mother-in-law and sister-in-law suggested that I give it some of the milk sweets we were carrying with us [to offer in worship].

So I did. I then turned, took one step, and looked back to see if the kitten was alright. It was nowhere to be seen. There was no kitten, no mewing, and no sweet. It had vanished. I couldn't understand this at all. I wondered if I had seen a vision. Who gave it to me?

Babul found herself pregnant the following month: "Then I realized that the goddess Sasthi had shown herself to me in the form of her animal carrier.[14] Siva and our gurudev had heard my vow and had accepted my faith and worship."

She followed up with further evidence that validated the unusual circumstances of her son's birth, and affirmed that indeed it was her guru who had been reborn to her:

Now, after this, I have observed many unusual things. For example, if I beat my son he falls very ill, more than some ordinary sickness. But he never gets angry with me when I beat him. He'll come and caress me, hang on my neck and ask for mercy, and fall on the ground like an adult. People are surprised to see him behave in this way. I myself realize I didn't do something right. So I don't beat him anymore. I'll scold him, but I won't beat him. I believe this in my *man.*

Babul followed with the story of her daughter, another child reborn to her, but interestingly, this is not their guru, who has been reborn already as her son:

My daughter too was born under unusual circumstances. I went back to the same Siva temple in Daksinesvar to make a vow. But this time the temple seemed lifeless—perhaps because my guru had already been reborn to me. So, before I left for the hospital [in her second pregnancy], I prayed to the picture of my grandmother-in-law to come to me as a daughter. I promised her that I'd serve her as her mother, if only she'd be reborn to me. If you call from your *man* you will be answered. I do believe my daughter is my grandmother-in-law reborn.

At this point Dinu commented that a disciple friend of his had already predicted this a long time ago to him, one day at the asram. He too "proved" this with similarities he found between his granddaughter and his mother:
"My granddaughter calls on the goddess Durga just as my mother used to. And if she finds my bed empty she asks where her 'baby' is."
Babul observed that her daughter was the first girl-child born to the family in a very long time, and that her father-in-law and her daughter were indeed extremely close, as if this connection had had its beginnings in a previous life.
In the accounts of experiences, the guru's own sakti is the context within which Kali's devotees, my participants, interpreted experiences related to initiation, healing, in posthumous connection, his instructions in dreams, and even his rebirth as a child into their family. It is a force manifested over time and space materially in two children (from two separate sources, the guru and the grandmother-in-law) born to a devoted supplicant. It is also manifested as the light surrounding a holy man (Sachin's experience on the plane). Resemblances between spiritually powerful individuals, as well as such symbols as matted hair (like Siva's), and a "wonderful" appearance provide a set of cultural meanings and connections that affirm the disciple's choice of guru, albeit with care, as Sachin's search illustrates. Both Dinu and Babul find confirmation of their faith in their guru's sakti, and concomitantly achieve at once a greater self-awareness. Dinu discovered that he had acquired the power to "heal" marriages in distress by absorbing the conflict into himself, much as his guru could absorb a disciple's illness and karma, noting to me that when he did this he would fight with his own wife, Bani—as if that which he had absorbed into himself

was consuming him in turn. Sachin too, found the power to heal a neighbor. Sakti, eternal, infinitely malleable, knows no boundaries, is transferred between persons, infuses objects, connecting and transforming. It is uncontainable and unbounded, as are, in participants' accounts, the guru's powers.

Such transformations in a disciple's sense of self are inspired less by a rational and progressive awareness (though this is obviously necessary) than by coming to know experientially who their guru "really is." The guru's own experiences, inspiring his own path of spiritual inquiry (in Sachin's story about his guru), legitimate his powers for his disciple. Subsequent experiences related to the guru then serve to consolidate the relationship within a culturally defined way of "knowing," continuing to effect transformations in disciples through their lives, even after the guru's death. Dinu observed to me that he had come to be more aware of his own true identity, his place in that larger scheme of things. Alokebabu's rhetorical question, "Who am 'I'?" finds a tentative answer in Dinu's comment: "I have seen myself, I have touched my atman."

NOTES

1. *Gurutattva o Gurugita*, in the *Visvasvaratantram*, v.7 and v. 18–20, Swami Raghubarananda ed. 1987.

2. Preface, *Gurutattva o Gurugita*, Swami Raghubarananda, ed., 1987; See also Swami Brahmananda (1987); Swami Budhananda (1991); Swami Sharadananda (1979); Swami Vivekananda (1982, 1992).

3. Mlecko too notes that the syllable *gu* means "ignorance," and *ru*, "he who dispels ignorance" (1982, 33).

4. From Vivekananda on the guru, in Raghubarananda (1987, 19).

5. From Vivekananda on the guru, in Raghubarananda (1987, 22).

6. Kohl (Bengali: *kajol*), made by burning clarified butter (ghee, itself the purest product of the cow, milk at its most refined, and used in ritual), is used cosmetically by women, but also has spiritual significance, enabling one to "see" with clarity. Silver containers containing kohl are often first gifts given to newborns.

7. Participants always referred to their gurus by this term, with honorific, as "guru-deity."

8. The Sivalingam, an aniconic form of the god.

9. A female preceptor is addressed as "Mother," Ma.

10. Kripal notes the relational "construction" of identity in reference to a holy persona, here Sharada Devi, where the devotee too is "constructed" as such in his or her perceptions of that persona (2001, 184).

11. This ritual, usually toward the end of formal worship, is seen as the "mouth" of the fire god, Agni, into which oblations are made, offerings which then reach the gods.

12. Evidently recounted by the guru to Sachin.

13. Saffron is the color of renunciation in Hindu belief, and interestingly, the color of the glow surrounding the holy man on the plane.

14. Sasthi is a Sakti goddess, giver of children, and their protector. Her "animal carrier" (*bahan*) is a white cat. Here Babul interprets the goddess metonymically in her animal.

Chapter 5

Alokebabu, Kali Devotee

A Guru as His Disciples See Him

In this chapter I describe my own "experience" of Alokebabu—not only as revealed in our conversations and his answers to my questions over my two phases of research, but also in his disciples' perceptions of him, and his powers. Several narratives, in different voices, including mine, offer, variously, perceptions of a man who is a reputed guru.[1] Only one brief account about his own possible powers is the story he himself would tell me, at the end and appropriately inconclusive in what it suggests. The first of four sections in this chapter presents my own conversations and perceptions of Alokebabu, his observations and commentary on himself as Kali devotee, and on devotion (bhakti) itself. The second section presents experiences of Alokebabu by visitors to his temple some of whom were his disciples. The third offers his story, in his voice. Finally, in the fourth section I conclude with a summing up of the themes which emerge across the different voices. Alokebabu's story finds context in my discussion of the persona of the guru in Hindu belief in the preceding chapter. Those speaking of Alokebabu frame their experiences of his powers in terms of indigenous concepts discussed in chapter 2, such as the *man*, and "intuitive knowledge," anubhuti, and the "power," Sakti, which the guru embodies, as he works to various ends (such as long-distance healing) by means of his "capacity," also sakti.

I first met Alokebabu in my first phase of research at his small Kali temple, a swarthy, heavy-set man in his mid-fifties or so. Over time he would confirm my first impression of an often-irascible, reticent, and sometimes impatient man, even with his disciples—despite the evident reverence, even awe, with which they regarded him. At my first meeting with him my father, introducing me and my research interests and requesting Alokebabu's assistance, said I would contribute to the free school he ran for poor children in the neighborhood. On my second visit, alone, to meet with him, the first thing the priest said to me, in sharp reprimand, was "I don't speak of my God for money!" I learned to be very careful around him, as much because I did not wish to bear the brunt of his tongue, as that I needed him as guarantor, for access to the Kali devotees who came to his temple. His disciples expressly referred to him as a man of learning, but also a Tantric practitioner, and one with powers beyond the ordinary, even as he himself briskly dismissed such claims.

I knew already that he had been a classmate of my younger paternal uncle at Calcutta (now Kolkata) University, and had a master's degree in Sanskrit. I would learn from devotees that he was married, but nothing about his family at this point (I did not breach his reticence). Bani, whose account appears later in this chapter (and her interactions with him, in chapter 6), would refer to his family's expectation that he pursue a career in teaching, that he had disagreed with them, and had, she said, "become separated" from his family.[2] A rare but telling comment by the priest himself about his mother comes up later in this chapter, and appears to explain his turn to his mother Kali. While Alokebabu the Tantric was closed to me—he was clear about this—I would find both Tantric and Kali devotee fluidly merged in the persona that I would come to learn about.

His expansive understanding of bhakti and Sakti/sakti was there for all to see in his temple. An eclectic group of humans, deities, and founders of religions, in framed prints and stone images, populated the wall facing the seating area within this small temple, the floor where visitors including myself would sit, as well in as the inner sanctum. There was a deity for everyone, but more. The sanctum (where he conducted rituals of worship) housed a three-foot-high black Daksina Kali,[3] dressed in a red Banarasi sari, with gold-plated silver ornaments on all four wrists, brass teeth, and protruding red tongue. She stood in front of a version of Kali as Tara, crowned with five skulls, holding a lotus in one of her four hands. Also in the sanctum stood the goddess Chinnamasta, with streams of blood streaming from her neck into her own severed head, which she holds in her hand. The sanctum had a two-foot-high Sivalingam, and to its right, Sani (Saturn), also a god in the Hindu pantheon. Behind the Sivalingam was an altar for the god Krsna and his female consort Radha. Stepping down from the sanctum to the seating area for devotees, to the left, stood a two feet high stone image of the meditating Buddha. On the right of this area, on the wall was a large blackboard, Alokebabu's schoolroom for the children of the neighborhood.

High on the wall directly facing the seating area and partially enclosing the sanctum hung a 12 × 12 inch framed print of Jesus of the Sacred Heart, in color, with small cameos depicting scenes from Christ's life (e.g., driving the moneylenders from the temple, the woman at the well, and the Last Supper). Other framed prints on the wall depicted an anthropomorphic

Siva, with a cobra coiled around his neck; Jagannath, Balaram and Subhadra (versions of the god Krsna and his brother and sister, respectively); and Hanuman, the monkey devotee of the god Rama, and a god himself. But other photographs depicted Subhas Chandra Bose, fiery Bengali revolutionary and hero of Indian resistance against the British; the late prime minister Indira Gandhi; her son, also prime minister, Rajiv Gandhi, both assassinated respectively in 1984 and 1991; and the Indian Nobel laureate for literature (1913), Rabindranath Thakur. I found of particular interest a framed photograph featuring American President John F. Kennedy and independent India's first prime minister, Jawaharlal Nehru, walking on the grounds of the White House.

I asked Alokebabu, why JFK? I could understand the possibly patriotic imperatives behind the revolutionary Bose, and the three Indian prime ministers. The presence of other divinities, besides Kali, were not unusual, as Hindus can and do pray to several deities, even as they hold a particular deity specially dear. Likewise, Jesus and the Buddha at a Kali temple were not that surprising, given a pervasive monistic concept in Hindu belief that divinity is one but has many expressions. But Alokebabu appeared somewhat surprised at my question, as if the answer should have been obvious. JFK (and Nehru) were possessed of sakti, as men of considerable ability, Alokebabu responded briefly to my question, without further comment. This evidently permitted JFK a place along with the other luminaries in his temple.

It is, perhaps, difficult to separate Alokebabu the man, from the devotee of Kali. Two incidents illustrate his impatience with those who might use his temple for purposes other than devotion. One hot afternoon as I sat on the floor talking with him, I noticed (for the first time) a small wooden plaque high on the wall to one side of the seating area, "banning" women. So what was I doing here, I asked him. He explained that he did not want women making the excuse to their families that they were going to the temple to worship, when in fact they were meeting up here with other women to gossip. I reflected that a certain misogyny did not conflict with the fact that this was a temple to a goddess! Another small sign proclaimed as "forbidden" the traditional and respectful salutations by touching the feet of elders or in this case, a guru. I would see him swiftly remove his feet in some irritation when a woman tried to touch his feet as she prepared to leave. I would learn later that Alokebabu was a diabetic, with an infected toe which one of his devotees, Gautam, a surgeon, would treat, as I had personally seen him do. I wondered if he simply did not abide by such obeisance, or whether he was protecting his infected toe. I don't have an answer. However, a formal notice forbidding this traditional and very common practice did give me pause.

I asked Alokebabu how he understood bhakti, the concept. He emphasized that a devotee has to "stake his right to God," *adhikar arjan karte habe,* he said, and repeated this. The devotee must assert, by the power and steadfastness of devotion, his indispensability to the deity. Such assertion obligates the deity to reciprocate, Alokebabu declared. In an interesting conflation of bhakti and sakti, Alokebabu offered as an example the relationship between the Krsna and his female consort and lover, Radha. Without Radha's devotion and her sakti, he said, Krsna's power is diminished, but with both, his power is enhanced. However, Alokebabu continued, integral to the feeling of devotion is the "ability," sakti, to reflect, to think on, and to act. These concepts were related, and not extricable one from the other, he asserted.

In a rare confidence, Alokebabu shared the following: "I see Kali as my 'live mother,' *jyanto ma*, because I never received the love and compassion from the mother who gave me birth. I don't know why I didn't."

He opened this door. In answer to my tentative questions, however, he replied that his human mother was alive, and that his older siblings did indeed get her love. He was the only one of his siblings who had chosen the "spiritual route," *adhyatmic path*. (I could only assume that this choice, and the more extreme, socially less acceptable one of Tantrism, had possibly been the cause of his rupture from his family). His choices, he said, seem to have been inspired when he had been initiated at age twelve or so (in his Brahman family). At this time, he said, "Something entered my *man*." But as he moved along that path of devotion, he had increasingly dispensed with ritual, and now simply sat quietly in his temple, knowing that his mother Kali "sees everything." Even when he performed the rituals at Kalighat Temple, he did not necessarily chant mantras, but simply asked his Mother to eat the food[4] offered to her, and to cast her "sight," *drsti*, on it.

Alokebabu observed:

> When my *man* desires, I offer flowers at Ma Kali's feet. But I don't do this because I want something from her. People who come to me say, call on Ma Kali, she will make you well. I know nothing. Just as a mother can understand a son's feelings, so can my Mother Kali. So I think.

When I asked Alokebabu if Kali appeared to him in dreams he said she did not, nor did he want to see the goddess in this way. He feared, he said, that if he saw the "true form" of divinity he might remove himself from the world, where he was needed. But, he added, again, "I know nothing." He simply kept his Mother Kali in his *man*, and asked her for nothing. So, at the end of the day, after people had left his temple, he said, "I shut the door and lie on the floor quietly. I know Ma is here, it is alright. Such thinking is faith." Otherwise, Alokebabu observed, he would be operating his temple "like an office," going home at the end of the day, having made a living from the foods and money his disciples donated.

In keeping with the requirement that a true preceptor be a person of impeccable integrity and rectitude, Alokebabu was particular in distancing himself from popular, and often justified stereotypes of rapacious and greedy Brahman priests (hence his early and sharp reprimand to me that he does not speak of his God for money). When I had asked him how he came to this "line" he mistook my English word to mean "line of income" (not vocation, as I had meant). He rebuked me sharply. "This is not a line!" he declared (also using the English word). He would elaborate on this comment at another time, observing that he had initiated many, but did not sell such acts of initiation, though small gifts of fruit and cloth are traditionally offered to a guru by the initiate. He was extremely skeptical of those who claimed to get diksa through dreams, declaring: "They have indigestion!" Those who aspire to learn, he said, need to be taught the alphabet.[5] This is the power of the guru, the teacher, who, like a doctor diagnosing a patient, is qualified to teach and to impart the mantra appropriate to the initiate. During this conversation, he commented that he saw me persevering at my work. So he had decided to speak with me, or, he added, he would have sent me on my way early on! He qualified this, however, and said that this might not apply to others, whose motives might be more self-interested. I took this as a compliment from a plainspoken, perceptive, and skeptical man. He advised me: "Call on the Mother, do your work, you will be victorious."

One evening, Rabindranath, a caretaker at Kalighat Temple, was at Alokebabu's temple as I spoke with the priest. He, like Debu (also a caretaker) followed a generational vocation to take devotees for worship at Kalighat Temple. Discoursing on Sakti, Rabindranath commented on the "huge" power which is given shape and form as Kali. As mother-love incarnate, he said, she is the ultimate shelter, where her devotee will be fed, find a place to rest, and to whom one can surrender.[6] Rabindranath "felt" (or "experienced") this power, he said, *anubhab kori*. His work, which he called a "weakness of his *man*," filled him with ananda, transcendent joy, which is inexpressible. It is Sakti which moved him to work for others. Alokebabu commented that it is this perception, an inner seeing, that sees Kali as beautiful and peaceful, beyond the "fearsome" power, Sakti, to which she gives (appropriately fearsome) form.

Regardless, I asked, is it not difficult to feel love for a mother of such terrifying appearance? Alokebabu said, indeed, this is not easy. But bhakti is not the simple love of a child for a mother whose care and compassion he (or she) can take for granted. Bhakti is learned, he said, beyond mere feeling. It requires effort, and thus, personal change. Such effort, ideally, is selfless, steadfast, requiring reflection and introspection, and not calling on Kali in times of trouble only, as so many who came to his temple do, he added. Thus, the true peace that such bhakti brings lies in one's own hands. He called this true devotion, and an "inner feeling." The devotee must persist in his quest, he continued, and without fear. Bhakti, ultimately is both an emotion but, as dedicated effort also an inner journey, *toward* a state of mind and being, thus a transformative process. Alokebabu offered as example Santosh, the musician who had been a part of the group of men with whom I had spoken (in chapter 2). There is a point where, after dedicated practice a musician rises above mere mastery of his instrument. This "essence" of a musical scale is transcendent of virtuosity, analogous to anubhuti, a higher perception.

In anecdote, some shorter and some more elaborate, Alokebabu's disciples and visitors to his temple spoke of, or implicitly suggested the powers of a man they evidently held in high esteem. Ananda, the other retired musician in the group we met earlier, described Alokebabu as both devotee and Tantric. He had gone with Santosh to meet the priest, and this first meeting had been "out of the ordinary." He had felt an instant "connection" with the priest. (Ananda, as an aside, commented that Alokebabu had been a wrestler in his youth, and had belonged to the same "lineage" of wrestling styles as himself). In 1976, sometime after he had been coming to Alokebabu's temple (after that first meeting) Ananda noticed that the holy water, *caranamrta*,[7] in the temple had alcohol in it:

> I drank it, and looked at the Mother Kali's face. I had drunk alcohol before, during my days as a musician, when I would play for princes. I asked Alokebabu one day, how do we look on Kali? As she who gives birth to the universe, we dress her, we feed her. If I drink alcohol in my [human] mother's presence, would this be appropriate? Alokebabu replied, "You are right," and after this he no longer added alcohol to his caranamrta. . . . Tantrics do this in solitude, [during rituals] at cremation grounds. But socially, this may be misunderstood.

When I naively asked Alokebabu early in my inquiries whether I could observe him at his Tantric rituals—which some had told me he performed, true to Tantric practices, at the Keoratala cremation ground, he brusquely refused and offered no explanation, ending any further discussion on the matter. When I said to Alokebabu that I had heard about his powers from his disciples, he staunchly and summarily denied this: "I don't do magic [*sic*]!"[8]

However, others saw him differently. One evening, in my second phase of research, while I waited at the temple for Alokebabu to arrive, a middle-aged woman, from the Marwari community of northwestern India, and also waiting for the priest, described him to me as a *siddhi baba*, a "realized" holy man, a Tantric practitioner of repute, and written about in newspapers—so she had read and heard. She told me, as we waited, that her daughter had married a Bengali (so, outside her social and caste group). Her son, deeply disapproving of the union, was abusing her with charges of prostituting his sister. She wanted Alokebabu to resolve her domestic troubles, and had come to the temple twice earlier that day to seek his help. Alokebabu was late in arriving. Two young men had been waiting with us. Alokebabu, showing up, brusquely asked the men why they had come to the temple. To get Siva's darsan, they replied (referring to the Sivalingam in the sanctum). Alokebabu said, "Well, you've had his darsan, now get out!" They left the temple, meekly, and without a word. I wondered how to read his evident brusqueness, what he knew that I did not. None of us present asked him to explain, or, I think, would have dared to.

Alokebabu himself maintained throughout that a devotee's faith in him did *not* imply *his* special powers.[9] At most, and at best, he said, he would supplicate his Mother Kali, who is "alive," jagrata, on their behalf. Evidently, he would decide whether the supplicant merited his request—based on something only he knew, and we did not.

However, Ananda offered an account of his own explorations into Alokebabu's "other" life as a Tantric:

> He does his own worship at night. So I told him, I will see where you go. Alokebabu asked me, can you? I replied, I will try. So, I sat in my room [at home]. With closed eyes, I saw him leave. He turned left. I could not get too close, something guarded him carefully. I decided to watch him from a distance. He went past a lake, and then on to the cremation ground. There were no people about. I watched his ritual, which I cannot describe, this is forbidden. Next day, I described my experience to him. He looked at me a long time, and said that I was 'exactly correct.'

Gautam, a surgeon in his early thirties when I first met him suggested that his meeting with Alokebabu had been predicted in a dream in which he had walked along a narrow lane which led to the banks of a river. However, he prefaced his meeting with the priest by speaking of his own mother, and a home where there had been an atmosphere of prayerfulness. He grew up hearing stories from the epics, like *Ramayana* and *Mahabharata*, of Vivekananda's influence, and reading Ramakrishna's words from the *Kathamrta*. He had asked, he said, the question we have met: "Who am 'I'?"

In his dream, Gautam continued, a small temple stood alongside the lane: "This is an unusual place for a temple, one does not expect to find it here, but I saw it before I started coming here. I consider myself blessed." There were times he "showed up" at the temple even if he did not intend to, unusually, since he lived some considerable distance away, in the north of the city. Coming to the temple, he said, focused his *man*. His "attraction" was Alokebabu himself, but he loved the Kali image at the little temple. Even though he had no "miraculous events" to share with me, Gautam commented that his readings of the *Kathamrta*, or Vivekananda's writings had contributed to his sense of intuition, anubhab, of Kali's presence when he had entered medical school. Now when he was at work, during a difficult surgery, or if there were post-surgical complications, "I think of the patient as deity, and proceed from there. If I can make him well I have achieved some kind of relationship with God. It is through work that I find God." He loved his profession, and aspired to do graduate work in surgical oncology.

Bani, whom I met with her middle-class, Brahman family at their home several times during both my phases of research, was a woman in her late fifties or so at the time. (We have met her husband, Dinu, her son Chandu, and daughter-in-law, Babul, earlier.)

Bani described her history with Alokebabu as a "relationship of long standing." She shared some details of his life, and her relationship with him in our conversations. The priest's father, also a priest, had presided at Bani's wedding, and served as the family's preceptor, for her paternal family line. Bani declared that she felt "great bhakti" for Alokebabu as a man of spiritual power. If he seemed distant on some days when she went to his temple, she meditated in silence. She valued his advice, and would be scolded by him if she did not go to the temple for some time, and she said, she would weep at his reprimand.

In support of her view of Alokebabu's spiritual status, Bani described an event that she "saw with her own eyes, she was there" on a visit to Alokebabu's temple with a woman friend:

"One day an impressive-looking non-Bengali man had come to [this] temple. The man's ninety-five-year-old guru lay critically ill in Almora [in distant Punjab state to the Northwest]. This man had asked his disciple to go to Kalighat Temple, to seek Alokebabu's help." (Bani implied that the Panjabi guru did not know the Bengali priest but had heard of his powers.)

Bani continued: "Alokebabu asked the Panjabi disciple to come the next day, and bring five kilograms of flour. The following day the priest set up the fire altar, and lit the fire. Then he told the Panjabi man, here are five *chapatis* [flat breads], which he pulled out of a bag."

I asked Bani, "Where did these chapatis come from?" Bani replied rhetorically, "Who knows?"

She goes on:

> Alokebabu then gave a piece of the bread to the Panjabi man, one to his another disciple who was there, ate part of it himself, and then threw the rest into the homa fire. "Go," he said to the Panjabi man, your guru will get back on his feet, and walk again, and eat chapatis!

Bani continued:

But as my friend and I watched, and as the homa altar was being taken out of the temple [the fire had burnt out, and the wood pyre on the altar had collapsed], I saw a six-month old infant lying on the homa altar. I asked my friend if she had seen this too. She said nothing. There are those who believe that if you speak of such things, you may never see them again. But surely if such things are true, why would we not say so?

"How did you understand what you saw?" I asked Bani. "Sakti connected the Panjabi guru and Alokebabu," she replied. She continued that only Alokebabu could save the ailing and distant guru, who must have had some karma[10] left, even at ninety five, which Alokebabu realized (with his special abilities). "But the child didn't have much longer to live. So Alokebabu took the child's remaining lifespan, perhaps five years, and transferred it to the ailing guru," Bani said.

"Was the transfer effected through the eating and burning of chapatis?" I asked. "Through Alokebabu, the Panjabi disciple, the other disciple who was present, the chapatis, and the fire," Bani responded definitively. She concluded that she could not express in words the power of the experience itself. This is anubhuti, Bani concluded.

When I met Alokebabu during my second phase of fieldwork he maintained, on the one hand, his impatience with those who sought his powers to address mundane issues, including those which were health-related. He was not running a clinic, he observed to me irascibly, they should see a doctor! If he could not know *his* own destiny, he could not predict this for others, he said. But he also described human agents of divine intent and purpose as yatri, "travelers" or "pilgrims," who serve divine ends. In retrospect, I think, he obliquely referred here to himself, and his powers, since this observation was followed by his recounting the following incident:

A pilot had come to me with problems related to passing his licensing exam, because he had a nagging ear problem. If he failed the exam he would not be allowed to fly. I had told him to not rely on "hocus pocus," *fusmantra*, and to see a doctor. I suggested he take two months' leave and get his ear properly treated. He did so, and returned, cured. He would pass his test.

Alokebabu continued:

"I ask, who directs this? I cannot explain this. But, that very day, my own ear started giving me trouble, it was infected and pus-filled by evening. I did not tell the pilot, or anyone else, since they would show up with medicine for me. Why is his ear cured, and mine now infected?"

Alokebabu moved his gray hair, and showed me the infection in his right ear. I did not ask if he would see a doctor himself, and he offered no explanation.

Where definitively knowing the ways of divinity amounts to human arrogance, both Alokebabu's careful skirting of such "knowledge," or any powers he might himself have, as well as my participants' own tentative interpretations of their experiences appears to be built into *how* these were recounted to me. At risk of a brisk dismissal, I would not ask Alokebabu for his version of events about his healing of the Panjabi guru at a great distance. Again, could he really "explain" the possible outcome of the rites he performed? But Bani's account was telling in what she included, how she explained what she saw "with her own eyes," her friend's silence about the apparent dead infant (which we can only assume that this friend saw as well), and her conclusion that she had possibly (how could one know for sure?) glimpsed at a "truth" briefly revealed as intuitive knowing, anubhuti—of Alokebabu's spiritual status, and related abilities, his sakti. At the end, we are left with questions, including about the chronology of events. I am assuming, based on what I observed about those who came to Alokebabu's temple that Bani and her friend had simply come that day, but that he might have mentioned the ailing guru across the country to her earlier. Whether in fact the Panjabi guru recovered seemed not to be the issue. The central point of Bani's account is, in the first place, her relationship of devotion with Alokebabu, whom she sees as a preceptor. From this premise follows her insight, anubhuti, into powers beyond the ordinary—the workings of Sakti—the transfer of life span to the distant guru from the dying or dead infant, seen in a waking vision. The medium of that transfer, the person capable of channeling Sakti, is Alokebabu. Also implied in this account is, the Panjabi guru knowing about Alokebabu's powers.

Alokebabu's fear of dreaming of Kali's "true form" suggests that dreams can indeed communicate some other reality, even as he dismisses diksa by dream as "indigestion." Ambiguity is built into the accounts, and such interpretation as I would hear about these. Alokebabu advises the pilot to get treated with modern medicine, even as his own healing powers seem to transfer the pilot's ear ailment to himself. Such accounts appears to suggest simultaneously the possibilities of what lies beyond ordinary human perception, as well as the impossibility of definitively knowing what such experiences *really* imply.

Alokebabu's question, "Who am 'I'?" even as the body perishes, remains, appropriately, unanswered. The journey to that answer is an ongoing one. Who really *is* Alokebabu? He lives in a world of social interaction, and of human suffering, and suffers from ill health himself. His disciples' evident respect and devotion for him and his own devotion for his Mother Kali is the premise across which human effort, sakti, and the mystery that is Sakti, that "huge power" given form as Kali, offers some context to his question, but not an answer, and appropriately so. If he is indeed, that "eternal" guru, given shape as a man, it is his disciples' accounts of glimpses, as anubhuti, of his powers that suggest such stature. Bani's "spiritual autobiography" involving several gurus, including Alokebabu, continues this theme in the next chapter.

NOTES

1. Alokebabu's reputation as a "realized" person would be confirmed in November 2020 by his successor at the Kali temple. I say more on this in the afterword.

2. I would learn more from Amlan Kanti Roy, son of Sri Rabindra Mohan Roy, in an e-mail dated November 3, 2020. Alokebabu had a son and daughter, whom he had educated. The daughter was married, and the son had not followed his father's vocation.

3. One of Alokebabu's disciples recounted to me the history of the Dakkhina Kali image. It had been thrown into the river Hooghly at Outram Ghat by a rich family down on its luck. The "boys" from Kalighat, seeing it in the water, would worship the image, with flowers and garlands. It would be submerged in high tide, and surface at low tide. When these young men told Alokebabu about it, he, thinking it to be a small image which he could install at the root of the banyan tree and Siva temple across from his temple, asked the men to bring it back. This took some doing, given the size of the image, said the disciple. Seeing how large it was, Alokebabu installed it, after repairs, in his own temple.

4. On the meaning of food offered to the Hindu deity, see Babb (1970); Khare (1977); Toomey (1986). *Bhog kara* is also "to experience." *Drsti bhog* is food offered to the deity, upon which she "casts her eye" (drsti), and thus consumes. Food offered in this context is then consumed by the devotee as prasad ("grace") in an act of communion. A female devotee described how, prior to the birth of her two children, she had dreamed that Kali had asked her to offer bhog. Living abroad at the time, she asked her mother-in-law in Kolkata to do so, at Kalighat Temple. Her two pregnancies and deliveries were "trouble free," and her children were now grown and doing well.

5. But see Kripal, on Ramakrishna teaching that an aspiring disciple could be initiated in a dream, the *svapna-siddha*, "dream-perfected" (2001, 180).

6. This is a common theme in the body of hymns to Kali, *syamasangit* (see McDermott 2001).

7. "Water from the deity's feet conferring immortality," imbibed by devotees after worship.

8. The risk of such experiences, perceived as "magic" was that they distracted from what Goswami (in chapter 2) would call the "real things," bhakti and bisvas, 'faith." He would distinguish "magic" from anubhuti, which was also "real." My

participants were wary of chicanery, and the egotism related to such displays. Tarun (in chapter 2) distinguished "magic" as lower on the path to realization, again because it involved an egotism that detracted from the true surrender of the self as required of the devotee. This is expressly stated in the commentary on the true guru's qualities (see chapter 4).

9. See Kripal on the "hermeneutics of hiddenness," where persons like gurus are "constructed" by "other people's interpretations" even when such persons themselves remain "silent" (2001, 172).

10. Here Bani means "destiny" by way of longevity.

Chapter 6

Bani's Many Gurus

Her Spiritual Journey to "Receiving" Kali

Alokebabu first introduced me to Bani at his temple with the words, "She is a great devotee (bhakta)." I met Bani in my first phase of fieldwork at her home not far from Kalighat Temple. Her immediate family, whom we have met in chapter 4, was her husband Dinu, her son Chandu, his wife Babul, and their two young children, who all lived in the same home. Bani was the third of four sisters, two of whom lived in Kolkata while one lived in Mumbai on the west coast. She had debilitating arthritis and suffered from occasional outbreaks of painful rashes on her body, a condition she had had for several years. She did not work outside the house, and, aided by Babul, saw to the running of the household. She had earlier been initiated by a Vaisnava guru, now no longer living, she said.

I posed my question to Bani, how do you understand Kali? She would recount a story involving experiences of and with various gurus, remembering and reflecting, of how she ultimately came to "receive" or "realize" her Mother Kali.[1] Bani told me her story at one long sitting.[2] It is full of questions, "experiences" which point to something larger, by implication but never with certainty. Unconcerned with chronology, this spiritual autobiography offers "events" along that journey as significant constitutive elements within the larger story—one of "realizing" Kali. In her style of telling, her narrative's reversals from present to past to present again, Bani hints at who she herself might really be (that quest, "Who am 'I'?"), a suggestion apparently (but never conclusively) supported and affirmed by her several gurus' words and actions (including those of Alokebabu). Her insights as dream events are recollected and connected in a non-linear narrative that finds continuities in retrospect. People with spiritual potential (her various gurus), and objects (like prayer mats and flowers) serve as springboards, mnemonic aids to free-associate and stitch together the many strands of the fabric of a life, still being woven when I spoke with her. Two parallel and analogous themes in the constitutive stories inform the progression and "plot" of the larger story. One theme tells of Bani's initial fear of Kali, and of her finally "receiving" or "realizing" what the goddess truly means. The other tells of her initial condition of "not knowing," of ostensibly fortuitous interventions by guru and/or deity, which she "receives" or which "happen" to her, for no obvious reason, intimating at, however, that larger truth. These interventions also hint at her own possible spiritual potential, or why would she receive the dreams, flowers, and mats so wonderfully and inexplicably gifted to her by spiritually elevated persons?

I myself was not extraneous to Bani's story but, it seemed, some part of the occurrences and events that were so meaningful to her, as someone who would record her recollections as smrti, as I discuss in my conclusion to this book.

GURUS WHO GUIDE AND
VALIDATE BANI'S JOURNEY

My question, following on from initially describing the broad parameters of my inquiry into the Bengali perception of Kali, whether Bani and her husband worship daily at home, is answered briefly in the affirmative. She says that she worships after a purifying bath and in a fasting state, only drinking cold milk and taking medication for her ailment. She prays on her prayer mat. Her mention of the mat launches her into the past, in which she recounts the miraculous gift in a dream of this mat to her from her beloved (first) Dada ("older brother," here a maternal cousin's husband), who, I learn later, had also first "given" her Kali. This account serves as prelude, as she emerges from the past to briefly observe that (now) she meditates on the goddesses Kali and Durga, and likes to do so, despite her early fears. After mentioning her prayer mat she begins:

> Then [after taking her medications] I put out my prayer-mat. My gurudev [her
> first Dada] gave me this mat. It was [first] received in a dream where he is call-
> ing to me: "Bani, I'm going to give you something. Keep it with care." Then I
> saw him holding out the mat to me. I awoke and felt very upset in my *man*. He
> was a great devotee, an "adept." My faith in him was enormous. . . . We used to
> visit Dada and his family every year at Kali's annual festival.

Bani comments, at this point, on Kali's presence and history in the family. Her maternal aunt, her Dada's mother-in-law, had "received" Kali in a dream, and had chosen to give the image to her daughter rather than to her son, who would not be able to "keep" such a fierce deity. This Kali image had stayed with Bani's cousin until her husband's death [the Dada Bani refers to], when it was given by the family to the Kali temple at Adyapith near Kolkata, ensuring its continued worship.

Bani then described the circumstances of her Dada's death. At his last illness, she went to see him "on the 21st." She told him about her dream (where he had given her his mat), at which he smiled but said nothing. He had not wanted her to leave but family needs forced her to, after she promised that she would come again to see him. "That night at 9:15" a phone call informed her that he had died. She continued:

> No one was home. My son had gone to the cinema, my husband was at the asram. I'm crying alone, you understand? I performed the last rites for Dada with Alokebabu, who looked at my Dada's photograph with concentration ["with his *man*"], and said to me, "He is a great adept, he will not be reborn." He had never spoken to me like this before. You understand the condition of my *man* at the time. I could not go to see Dada, couldn't do anything for him [before he died]. . . . One must perform one's gurudev's last rites . . . I performed these on that mat at Alokebabu's temple.

She now remembers her other (initiating) guru's mat which she also possesses, and places under the mattress on her bed. This was given to her by this other guru at an earlier date, which she does not specify. She describes the circumstances of her initiation in the town of Gaya, (a pilgrimage town in north-central India). The guru took her to a beautiful temple to Kali at the foot of a hill. Here he uttered the secret seed-incantation in her ear, despite the fact that she was not in a fasting, therefore ritually pure, state:

> This is a secret thing about my life—I'm telling you for the first time . . . Dada gave me diksa sitting in that mountain cave. As soon as he did, I forgot the mantra. I asked him, "What did you say? You said so much, I remember only a little." He whispered in my ear again, and said, "It doesn't matter, you can say whatever you remember. Afterwards, keep repeating it. If you forget, I'll remind you."

Bani said that her *man* was disturbed because her initiation had not been accompanied by traditional rituals such as the fire ceremony, new clothes and celebration, and that her "fate" seemed always to be different from that of others.

She now recounted her experience with Rangama, a female preceptor, who lived near Kalighat Temple:

> But in my life, whether from my Dada [her cousin's husband], whether from my guru [also Dada, in Gaya], whether from Rangama—that which I have got

from Rangama, that is through a dream. I had not gone to her. She lives in this neighborhood. She is a *sadhika* [a female adept], very well known. She lived with Anandamayima.[3] She too has a God-gifted [*sic*] thing.

But I wanted to know the rest of the previous story, and asked what happened after her guru gave her the seed-incantation. She replied:

After I received my diksa, my gurudev seemed to know about my son's illness in Calcutta. He told me that my child would get better, which he in fact did. As I came down the hill, he reminded me once again of the mantra. He said, "You can do it, keep chanting the mantra. Do the best you can." Indeed, while descending I found myself remembering some of the mantra . . . I was myself surprised. Then, he said to me that he would help me, should I forget the mantra, and that I shouldn't worry.

I asked her to explain the meaning of the initiation mantra and the guru's role. She elaborated:

That mantra in which you ought to be initiated, he who understands this, he is the guru . . . he can give it to you only after he understands your "*man's* words" [words which are inner and secret]—that you are the devotee of this or that particular deity. If you tell him and he gives it to you—then there is nothing to it. He has to understand what you want, that you love this particular deity, that you secretly want this deity in your *man*. He can initiate you with that mantra only after he understands this.

Bani asks rhetorically, "What is the meaning of diksa?" She answers her own question. "Suppose you are a devotee of Siva. If you get Ma Kali's mantra, will you like it? No, you won't. Suppose you like Siva and also Krsna. That the guru must understand."

Bani illustrates her comments at this point on initiation and the abilities of this guru with another remembered story:

When I was young, I loved Krsna. I was afraid whenever we went to Kalighat Temple. My grandmother used to take me there, but I did not like it. I liked it at the Krsna temple there [within the Temple precincts]—they give holy water there. And Siva—with my child's *man* I loved him. During the Second World War my father had kept us with my cousins. They would bully me, saying if they didn't win when we played they would beat me. If they won they promised to feed me sweets. I used to pray to Krsna in my *man* and when they won, I used to be very happy. But when Dada [the guru in Gaya] gave me diksa I asked him, what does it mean, that which you have given to me? That I would get what I love! Truly, in my life—I speak from my *man*—I loved Siva so much, I loved Krsna so much!

So faith was born in my *man*. Even at a young age. This did not go away as I grew older. So with Siva—I used to be taken to worship him. I used to say nothing—I used to hug [his image] and adore him. There is a Siva in clear water there near the banks of the river Ganga. And when my gurudev gave me the mantra, he did so because he understood all this. I asked him, much later, what is the meaning of the mantras given to me? He said, "Tell me, Bani, is this not what you love?"

She interjects her story with the comment, "But see, when I recite Kali's mantra, or Ma Durga's mantra, I now like it."

COMING TO KALI

I asked if Kali comes later into her life. Bani replied that she had, though her first Dada had "given" her this deity. However, she was afraid of Kali and especially disliked the animal sacrifices at Kalighat Temple and at her in-laws' home. I prompt her, given that I know now that she has come to "like" Kali.

At this point Bani relates another dream, this time of Kali herself, but more ambiguously, hinting at possibilities rather than at certainties (such as her unqualified love for the gods Krsna and Siva):

I myself did not know about Tarama [the version of Kali at Tarapith Temple]. One day I'm dreaming that—when I told Alokebabu he stared at me in surprise—I said, "I didn't understand the meaning of this, that's why I'm asking you. Why are you staring at me?"

Since she had jumped ahead to describe Alokebabu's reaction to her dream and to seek his validation, I return Bani to describe her dream. She continues:

I'm dreaming that Ramakrishna, my [Gaya] gurudev, and Loknath Baba who is Siva himself[4] . . . I am in my *man* as if unconscious. Loknath Baba is sitting next to me, fanning me and putting cold water compresses on my head. I am quarrelling with Ramakrishna and saying, "Why must one call upon you for so long before you answer? Why do you reveal yourselves only when people suffer? Can parents bear their children's suffering?" Ramakrishna is looking at me, but not saying anything. Loknath Baba gave me some *sinni* [a sweetened liquid], and asked me to drink it. As I speak to you, I can see that vision before my eyes. My domestic help then awoke me, I received a shock [*sic*].

Bani continues:

When I could walk, I went to see Alokebabu. I told him that when I had been ill I had had a dream. I remember clearly what I saw though I don't understand it. He said, "I don't know anything," and started going up the stairs [to the inner sanctum in his temple]. I said, "I'm telling you *because* you don't know about it." He said, "People practice [spiritual discipline, sadhana] for eons and don't receive this, and you have received it just simply lying in your room. And you have come to ask *me*?!"

    From then on, whenever I suffer I remember my dream. . . . A faith was born in my *man*. At times . . . I smell a fragrance—it is a sign. I advise people to do or not do something. I find that I am right. I don't know why this happens.

Bani reverts to an experience related to Rangama, the woman preceptor whom she had briefly mentioned earlier.

One day, I'm dreaming that I was returning from Kalighat Temple. My gurudev and my son were traveling by rickshaw. "Where are you going?" I asked. They said, "To the Temple." Ma Kali had asked my son in a dream, "Can you make me a nose ring?" He had said, "Yes, I will." All this I saw in the dream. I know nothing at all. See, I never went to Kalighat much—sometimes on Tuesdays or Saturdays—my son used to be frequently ill, that's why I went. I used to, it's true, come home with peace in my *man*. One day I dreamt Ma Kali is saying to me, "You, come to me, take this flower, keep it with you. Whatever you want, I will hear you." Rangama was there in the dream.

I asked Bani to tell me more about Rangama. Bani emphasized this woman's importance, and that the daily morning rituals at Kalighat Temple began only after she went there. She then observed that she herself had never gone to see her at her asram though Rangama had stopped by her house on her way to Kalighat Temple. Now, however, on the insistence of a friend, Bani visited her and told Rangama about her dream.

After receiving this dream I went regularly to see Rangama. She laughed, and said, "So you have received such a dream. From where did Kali give you so much?" 'Why did I see this?' I asked her. She said, "Today I can't come to see you but tomorrow you will bathe, wear clean clothes, and I will bring you a flower from the Temple." Rangama is manifest Daksina Kali herself.

I asked Bani to explain.
She said that Rangama had miraculously appeared to her disciples simultaneously at her asram, and at Kalighat Temple, so she had heard. She waited

from 6 to 9 a.m. with no sign of Rangama. As soon as she began to feed fish to her young and hungry niece, Rangama arrived at her home. Since by touching fish Bani had become ritually polluted Rangama went to the home altar herself and placed the red hibiscus flower from the Temple in a stone bowl. This was in 1971 or so, Bani replied in answer to my question. That flower was with her still. She continued, asking a rhetorical question and then answering it herself:

> After that, I have been with my Ma Kali. What is the Mother like?
>
> My son was very ill, with typhoid. Rangama went to the Temple, picked up some flowers kept near the image there and gave these to me to place at my altar—instructing me to keep them there till they dried. "When he improves, float them in the Ganga," she said. My son's health improved. Rangama never told me not to go to a doctor or get medicine.

Bani concludes:

> In my life these three people have made so great a difference. No rituals. I never asked—things came of themselves. Rangama used to ask me to visit her, saying, "I have some things to talk about with you. Things which can only be talked about when there are not too many people around. One cannot speak of one's inner thoughts to everyone." She never took any money from anyone. She disliked being given things. She was very particular about her ways. . . . She and Anandamayima were as one. We remembered Namdev. . . .

Bani went on to tell me about her "receiving" Kali as Tarama, returning in her story to Tarapith temple, where the saint Namdev had performed his meditations. The dream's prediction was fulfilled when Bani visited Tarapith and saw that Kali image for the first time. She spoke to Alokebabu about her dream. He told her that her good work (sukrti) in some previous life was probably yielding its fruits. She continued:

> So I said [to Alokebabu], "My life's spent just looking after the family." He said, "This is the real thing. In the midst of this, you will learn." Rangama used to say, "The person who can be an ascetic in the midst of *samsara* [both 'world' and 'family'], is great. It is not so difficult to be a yogi alone in the Himalayas. When in spite of the world's demands you call on God—this is great sadhana. Nothing is obtained without such discipline."

Bani's remembered experiences appear to have some quality of transcendence over the natural, everyday logic of things and events in space and time. They are appropriately, then, placed in a narrative structure that is uninterested in actual historical or linear continuity, with factual gaps (she doesn't mention when her first Dada gave her the prayer mat, or the Kali given by his mother-in-law). While a journey loosely and ostensibly in time and in space, it is also an inner one in her *man*, of deities she has loved in her youth, and which her initiating guru (in Gaya) intuits with his powers, proven in his accurate intuition, and the appropriate seed-incantation he gives her. It is her *man*'s secret, inner words and desires that he understands. Her cousin's husband, an adept validated by Alokebabu, also understands something about Bani, offering her his prayer mat in a dream, and which she now possesses. Her connection with him too transcends the familial relationship, but is one in her *man* where she suffers and weeps when unable to be with him at his death. The various gurus do not expect material remunerations, as Rangama explicitly says. They "know" about her ailing son and predict his recovery. Dreams, even dreams within dreams like that of her son being asked by Kali for a nose ring, communicate these inner connections—including with the saints she berates in her dream when she is unwell, of being lax as "parents." Rangama, the female adept, is Kali herself according to Bani. Once Bani has made contact with her (after Kali instructs her in a dream to get a flower from the Temple, a dream where Rangama was present), this female adept brings her the flower, a red hibiscus—itself a metonymic representation of Kali, a flower which has remained with Bani over the years. Rangama also wants to speak with her in private, suggesting that this saintly woman sees some potential in her—as evidently her first Dada, her initiating guru in Gaya, and Alokebabu do as well. Kali's special saints who provide succor in her dreams, Ramakrishna and Loknath Baba, affirm, by their presence in her dream, but by implication only, Bani's accumulation of merit over many lives, her possible earlier "good work," her own potential. As Alokebabu asks rhetorically when she describes her dream to him, why ask *him*, when *she* has "received so much?"

Bani omits any mention of the years related to the events she recounts though she may be particular at times (the phone call at 9.15 about her Dada's death). It is I, the ethnographer, who has attempted some measure of "logic" in presenting Bani's journey to "receiving" Kali, and suggest that the association of events, as dreams, or in actuality, have a spiritual continuity, not a temporal one. Her comments on her own "not knowing" what a dream portends, why she received diksa without its formal requirements (in Gaya), even that Alokebabu claims not to know the meaning of her dream about Kali's saints Namdev and Ramakrishna, suggests the uncertainties of her "journey" and its inconclusiveness—by definition, given who is being sought, and who may be ultimately knowable, here Kali herself. In Bani's story, the miraculous is ever-present, and waiting to be seen as such. Kali's image, given to a deserving daughter by her aunt, Bani's cousin, begins her account. Bani's story ends with a dream from Kali as Tarama, and her seeing this image at Tarapith temple. She "now" no longer fears Kali.

NOTES

1. Bani said both "*ami Ma Kalike ki kore pelam*" ("how I received the Mother Kali"), or "*ami Ma Kalike ki kore upalabhdhi korlam*" ("how I realized the Mother Kali").

2. I have edited and on occasion paraphrased parts of Bani's story, but have retained her free-associative style, interjecting only to bring her back to some story she begins, but moves on to another.

3. A renowned woman saint (1896–1982). With this association Bani validates Rangama's spiritual mentor.

4. A reputed saint, born 1790, who reputedly lived until 1830.

Chapter 7

Devotional Practices and Experiences

Accounts of miraculous experiences are related to different contexts in devotees' lives and devotional practices. These take various shapes ranging from semi-biographical to more autobiographical, longer and sequentially structured, or shorter and anecdotal. I present select accounts in this chapter by eight devotees, five women and three men. The contexts for the experiences are understood within a devotee's choice of religious practice and relate to the conceptual flexibility of devotion as Bhakti. Devotees' reflections on Kali, on Bhakti, and on Sakti are woven into their stories and their interpretation of their experiences. Symbolic motifs, and substances and objects used in worship illustrate, in keeping with Bhakti's flexibility, a proclivity to dispense with definitive boundaries, such as the red hibiscus flower offered to Kali as metaphor for the self/*man* of the devotee, in ritual and in hymn. The miraculous itself, understood variously, ranges across a spectrum from the inexplicable, such as a devotee who sees bright lights without obvious source, to the apparently so (e.g., a child healed when Kali is supplicated). Humans too appear as agents in the accounts, directed by divine will, for example in Abhijit's account, who first has such an experience only when he is with his devout sister-in-law; a mysterious holy man who predicts a resolution of a life crisis for Ananda; children who appear, disappear and reappear when Sumona offers food to Kali; and Nandita's father who saves a stranger from suicidal intent. A devotee may interpret an experience as offering an intuitive insight, anubhuti, into the mystery of the deity's workings, as also a gift given by divine compassion. Such "gifts" are also interpreted, in their unpredictability, as Kali/Sakti's divine "play." The reputed Bengali poet and composer Qazi Nazrul Islam (1899–1976) describes the Hindu divinity as a gigantic infant, unpredictable and arbitrary, utterly absorbed in [her] "mind" as [she] "plays" with the world.[1] While the devotee's journey to "know" divine mystery may

involve various paths, interpretations of experiences, involving as these do
the ultimately unknowable, end in questions, and assertions that such experiences are beyond logical comprehension, and beyond human explanation.

Appropriately, given the open-ended understanding of Bhakti, ritual practices themselves, which may be prescribed in prayer manuals, are ultimately
a matter of personal choice, where some devotees dispense with worship
involving the offering of objects and substances at the home altar or at the
Temple. They may favor instead more solitary practices requiring none of the
above, meditating instead—at Temple, at home, or even on a daily morning
walk. Some devotees incorporate at the start of their account a history of how
they came to be devotees of Kali. The personal or familial daily rituals performed by devotees are, then, variously a matter of family traditions, personal
choice, or inspired by some "event" which may be on a spectrum, interpreted
as being beyond the ordinary. Such choices of ritual practice are described as
"an affair of the *man*," *maner byaper*, and are deeply personal. A worshiper's
ultimate rationale, however, is what he or she "loves" to do, a feeling in the
man. Acts of, for example, offering foods, or flowers to the goddess at the
Temple or at the home altar are ultimately a free choice, happily done, even
if a family tradition. This flexibility and conceptual malleability translates to
ritual objects and actions. Items used in worship, for example vermilion or
the red hibiscus, as metonyms for Kali/Sakti, and symbolic themes in ritual
action such as adoration with lit oil lamps, *arati*, are woven into accounts of
experiences, and give meaning to the accounts to follow.

Red is the color of Sakti, and appears ubiquitously in substances used in
Kali's worship, symbolizing simultaneously the immanent as well as transcendent deity. Red celebrates the goddess as Creatrix, life giver, even as the
color suggests the "undefeated" transcendence over the sort of "death" that
attachment to the world, to life, and to sexuality imply.[2] The color red is also
"auspicious," *mangalik*, a concept particularly associated with the creative,
life-giving powers of the Sakti goddess. Kali is appropriately "the embodiment of mangal."[3] The goddess is offered vermilion as paste or powder, red
sandalwood paste, the "blood-red hibiscus," *raktajaba*, but also purple flowers called *trijoni* ("three vaginas," also called *aparajita*, the "undefeated").[4]
In hymns to Kali the *man,* thus the devotee himself, is conflated with the red
hibiscus as an offering of the self to the deity. A composition by Qazi Nazrul
Islam asks the hibiscus "what spiritual discipline it had practiced to earn it a
place at the feet of the Mother," a metaphor for the devotee seeking refuge.
Ramprasad sings of the devotee's *man* as the red hibiscus, offered in surrender to divinity:

Man, become the hibiscus at my Mother's feet!
. . . *Man*, don't forget your compassionate Mother

Her blood-covered form will be your refuge;
Man, at those dark feet, surrender yourself entirely;
Man, become the hibiscus at my Mother's feet![5]

Symbolic motifs on the Kali icon related to perception and "seeing" point to the journey the worshiper needs to undertake as he or she aspires to see beyond the world of finite Time and all that lives in it. These include the third and "inner" eye on Kali's forehead, the "center of consciousness" and sixth locale (of seven) along the body in yoga, with which one "sees" rather than merely "looks." Kali's "sword of knowledge," which she wields in her upper left hand (of four arms) severs "bad knowledge" or "ignorance," represented by the demon's head she holds in her lower left hand. Rituals of adoration at worship's beginning, *mangalarati*,[6] and at end, arati, where the worshiper or priest waves a lit oil lamp in front of the image, likewise symbolize perception and enlightenment (See Figure 7.1).

A love for the act of worship involving the many substances used in ritual (food, flowers), temple visits and other actions are broadly described by devotees as "outer," or more "ritualistic," *anusthanik*. The act of meditation is distinguished as "inner," *bhetorer byapar*. However, each kind of ritual action incorporates the other, since the *man* is the originator of both choices, which are not exclusive, and a matter of preference for the devotee. The

Figure 7.1   The Ritual of Arati, Adoration. *Source*: Photograph by the author.

"outer" revels in beauty—in the offerings to Kali, such as the red hibiscus, the fragrance of incense, the sound of prayer chants, the rich lyrics and music of syamasangit, hymns for Kali composed by her saints, like Kamalakanta and Ramprasad Sen—even as all these simultaneously express, and point to, the beauty of the "inner." So, participants describe their "joy," ananda, in acts of worship involving "outer" actions, and describe such "attraction" as "the mother Kali showing herself in their *man*."

The male and female devotees whose stories follow are diverse in their socio-economic backgrounds, in their histories as related to Kali's worship, as well as in religious practice. Their accounts of events are necessarily diverse, sharing however in their interpretive paradigm concepts of Bhakti, Sakti, "intuitive knowing," anubhuti, and the *man*. I have grouped four accounts, three by a young woman, Nandita, and one by a middle-aged man, Abhijit, as they share a theme of experiences associated with proximity to other devotees. Sumona expressly speaks to her wondrous experiences in relation to her love of offering foods to her Mother Kali. Ranu, educated in Catholic institutions India and at Purdue University in the United States, is a devotee of Kali but with a casual interest in ritual. Manju and Deb, a married couple in their thirties and forties, with very different ritual practices, both initially claim no miraculous experiences, but ultimately on reflection, do. Ananda, advised by a mysterious holy man to meditate daily on the goddess, is able to emerge from his financial hardship and provide for his family. I end with one story different to the others. Bimala, with a long family history of Kali worship and her own intense religious practices but dismissive of the miraculous who turns to atheism when her prayers fail to keep personal tragedy at bay. The men focus on meditation practices, again variously—a daily walk to Kalighat Temple over decades (Abhijit), remembering deities and ancestors on a morning's walk (Deb), or chanting a particular incantation of praise from the *Devi-Mahatmya* (Ananda). In the conclusion of this chapter I offer my reflections on the particularities of the accounts, as well as the unifying theme which connects the narratives—one of transformation, in the self of the participant, in his or her life, in another way of "seeing" which such anubhuti afford.

EXPERIENCES IN PROXIMITY TO OTHER DEVOTEES

I met Nandita, a married woman in her late teens, and her aunt-in-law, Manju, at the latter's beautiful home in south Kolkata, on the occasion of a performance by their hymn-singing and charitable group, *Mangalik*. Nandita's own claim to the possibly miraculous was that her voice would be "somehow" alright even if she had had a cough before she would sing at worship at their temple, or at Mangalik's performances. Another female relative, a sister-in-law, present for this weekly event, commented that many "events" had occurred at Nandita's paternal home (in north Kolkata), and observed that these events were anubhuti, and "extraordinary," adbhut. Nandita was initially reluctant to share the accounts, fearing that I was a journalist and would sensationalize them. I assured her that I was not a journalist, and that her stories spoke to my research interests, and merited my respect.

The clay image of Kali, Nandita began, had been ritually established at the small temple on the ground floor of her parents' home, and was worshiped every new moon (auspicious to Kali), by her father and three brothers. "In our family, Kali is most precious . . . our family is one of devotees," she observed. Before she recounted the events at their temple, and to illustrate her point, she spoke about her older brother, her Dada.

He had a heart condition, Nandita began, had recently undergone an ECG procedure, and been advised rest by the doctor. He would normally perform the concluding (and physically demanding) rite of adoration, arati, at the celebration of Kali's annual festival at their home temple. In the circumstances, she continued:

> Because he so desired to do arati he just asked for a lighter bell and horsehair whisk [waved around in this rite]. But by the end of arati he collapsed and had to be taken to the hospital. On his return and on the day before the Mangalik performance he lay upstairs and watched all the activity [on the ground floor]. He had wanted to do arati that day as well but we all scolded him. Ma Kali was being adorned, it was as if she wanted her devotee to see this, and was pulling him to her. He could hear the bells ringing, the sound of the *shehnai* [Indian clarinets]. . . . This is the "draw," *tan*, between God and devotee.

Nandita elaborated: That my brother could not participate, he suffered in his *man*. We could not really comprehend[7] his suffering. Ma Kali wants her devotee to see her being adorned—this is an understanding between the two. So I don't blame him. Ma Kali has attracted him to her. It is by her will that she has shown herself in his *man*." Nandita cited Ramakrishna to make her point: "A bird can say 'Radhakrishna' until a cat catches it by the throat. So a man can utter the name of God but when he is in physical pain, he forgets it. But my brother even when critically ill had no other word but the name of the Mother on his lips."

With this prologue, and setting the scene, Nandita then continued with three more accounts, in succession, of unusual events at her home, all related to her devotee parents. Each involved the apparently serendipitous advent of people to the family's temple, one to rectify a ritual lapse, one (possibly) seeking succor, and the third, an unbeliever, taught a lesson in faith by no less than the saint Ramakrishna himself in a dream. Nandita briefly interpreted these events not only in terms of her family of devotees, but also in terms of the Mother Kali who knows what is in her devotee's *man*. She concluded with the unpredictability of Sakti, which works to direct events, toward its own ends, a power beyond human understanding and logic, but one which is—implicitly—ultimately compassionate and protective.

Nandita proceeded with her first account:

One day, a young, unmarried[8] girl came to our house, and stood at the open door of our temple, watching my father arranging and decorating the deities inside. Then she came straight upstairs. My mother was surprised, and asked her who she was.

She replied, "You don't know me, and I don't know you either. However, I have come here without knowing you or your house. Why I am here, I do not know. I was on my way to [another Kali temple in north Kolkata] by tramcar. For some reason I cannot explain, I got off at a stop where I should not have. I don't know this area, but I started walking as if I did. I came, as if directed, straight to the gates of your house, saw the temple, and entered."

My mother asked, "However, why are you here?"

The girl answered, "I was going to the other temple to put vermilion on the Mother. But since I am here, if you give me your permission, I will offer my gift of vermilion at this temple. I must have been directed to do this by the Mother, otherwise I cannot explain my presence here at all."

My mother asked her to go ahead, also telling my father why the girl had come. My father was most amazed, and welcomed her into our temple. The girl put vermilion thrice on the goddess, offered salutations, and left.

After she had gone, my father burst into tears. He said that he would normally put vermilion on the deity every day without fail. For the last two days, because of various distractions he had forgotten to do this remembering after he had closed the temple for the night. He had forgotten yet a third time [today] when the young girl showed up and put the vermilion on Kali.

Nandita commented in conclusion:

"It is obvious how the Mother is everywhere, that she knows her devotees' *man*. How wonderful are her ways of getting things done!"

Nandita then recounted another incident, also related to her father:

On another occasion, my father saw a middle-aged woman sitting in front of our temple and crying. She looked well-off, she wore a lot of jewelry, and she was beautiful. My father asked her, "Why are you weeping like this? Come upstairs, the temple is now closed, I can't open it yet."

But the woman did not go upstairs. She said, "Why I came here I don't know. I was going to the [river] Ganga. I don't know these roads. I'm not used to walking these roads alone. . . . But I see that the temple is closed."

My father asked, "If you were going to the river why didn't you go there? Who is with you? You don't look like you are accustomed to walking alone. Why are you out alone like this on the streets?"

The woman lowered her head, "I was going to the Ganga to commit suicide. I lost my way and showed up here. I don't know where the river is, I saw the temple and came into your home."

My father said, "Obviously Ma Kali must have known you were committing an unholy deed, which is why she brought you here and made you stay. Don't make this mistake again. You have been stopped in an inauspicious act. How the Mother must have been hurt in her *man* to bring you and keep you here!"

"My father," Nandita said, "didn't ask the woman her problem, but he felt[9] that she would not attempt suicide again. He then saw her to the main road, as she left."

Nandita's third account described an "event" related to her mother:

My mother's professor of English [when her mother had been studying in college] was a Dr. M. He was not religious, so it seemed. He did not give the impression of either believing or not believing in God. In his manners and ways, he was most Anglicized. He knew my mother was quite the opposite and would laugh at her, saying that she knew nothing but her goddess, and Ramakrishna. My mother was not a young woman at this time, she was very spirited, and retorted freely to his taunts.

One day, just as mangalarati was over in our temple, our servant ran upstairs to tell us that Dr. M. was here. We were surprised, since it was very early. When we went downstairs, he requested that the temple doors be re-opened, as he wanted to offer salutations to Kali, and to Ramakrishna [whose picture hung on the wall]. He entered, then prostrated himself in front of Kali's image.

[Afterwards] we asked him, "What happened, sir? Why are you here so early?"

He replied, "I am guilty of a great wrong. I must ask the Mother for forgiveness before I speak with you." He stayed a few minutes at the temple praying silently, then came upstairs with us.

He told us: "I don't know how to describe my experience. As the night was coming to an end, I dreamt that Ramakrishna stood in front of me, a brilliantly lit form. The waves of light hurt my eyes. He said, "Come with me." I asked, "Where?" He replied, "Follow me, and you will find out." He took me down College Street, then down these streets of [north] Kolkata. I kept asking where he was taking me, and he answered as before. He finally led me to your house, and your temple. The temple's doors opened, and he merged with the picture of himself [on the wall].

"As soon as I awoke, I wore the first thing I could find and ran here. I did not even take the tramcar. Thakur had brought me here walking, and I thought I could get here more quickly if I ran."

Dr. M. continued:

You think Ramakrishna stays in your temple? He is everywhere, he cannot be shut in.[10] Perhaps I hurt her [referring to Nandita's mother] in some corner of her *man* with my teasing. She is a great devotee, but she did not express her hurt because I was her teacher. So he [Ramakrishna] came to call me. Because of her I had such a wondrous anubhuti. What good had I perhaps done in a previous life? [Ramakrishna] showed me that he is alive. There are so many temples around—why did he bring me to this one, which is her home?

Nandita concluded:

Dr. M. wept. For the kind of man he was, this event was utterly extraordinary.

I asked Nandita how she understood such experiences. She replied rhetorically:

Such things are not amenable to rational explanation, or logic. Sakti indulges in such wonderful acts, manifesting her "light."[11] Such occurrences are anubhav, matters of the inside. . . . Who is moving me? It is Sakti. You can call it God [bhagavan], or anything. Again, you might want to do something and you are unable to do so—what stops you? What directs you? Our "intelligence," buddhi, cannot find the logic, cannot explain. It is unpredictable, sudden. I'm calling this God, and Ma Kali, but this is Sakti at work. When a loved one dies, it follows that someone brought (him) in, and then takes (him) away. That is Sakti. I can do nothing about death. I cannot grasp at this Sakti, it is beyond my capability. I don't understand, yet something gets done.

Abhijit's experience, of a bright light which appeared to be without source, is associated with a devotee, his older brother's widow. It was an experience that initiated a life of dedication to Kali. He claimed no other "experiences," however. He understood his contentment itself with what he has in life as something given to him, by his Mother Kali's compassion.

A married man in his fifties when I first met him at his home, and a secretary to a judge in Kolkata's court system, Abhijit described his sister-in-law as a "great devotee." He had not been particularly religious-minded, he said. But his sister-in-law, although an uneducated woman, read "a lot" in Bengali and Sanskrit, her father had been a scholar, and she herself was a knowledgeable person on religious matters. On a visit to see her, as they were talking, she suddenly asked if he could see the powerful light falling on a framed saying by Ramakrishna which hung on the wall of the room. Abhijit, then about twenty or twenty-one years old, was skeptical. He checked from where he was in the room and saw nothing. His sister-in-law then asked him to come over to her side of the room. Here, he saw a bright light which then gradually faded. He searched for a source, but could not find any.

When I asked Abhijit to describe the light, he replied, "like a ball of fire." However, he added that the light he saw had little to do with him. It was because of a devotee, his sister-in-law, and her compassion that he was able to have this experience.

At the time, nothing else changed for him. Then he took his Bachelor's examinations, and failed them. Prior to his second attempt, on the advice of a cousin who suggested that on his daily morning walk he go by Kalighat Temple, he did so. He passed his exams, one of the 14 percent of students who did. He supplicated the goddess with help finding work—the day he offered worship at the Temple, he got a job, all with "Ma Kali's compassion." From then he had been going every day to the Temple, and "really loved going there." However, Abhijit offered just salutations as a rule at the Temple, and did not perform rituals. He also didn't have the money to spare to purchase items to make offerings. His faith was then further confirmed when a long period of ill health ended, after he had again implored the goddess. Others who knew him, he said to me, described such steadfast devotion over the years since as an act of "spiritual discipline," sadhana. What he wanted from Kali now is that his *man* stay on her, Abhijit concluded, then he would find peace. No, he responded to my question, he did not see the goddess in dreams, nor did he believe in getting initiated by a guru. He had not found a guru he could trust. Nor did he offer blood sacrifice, which he considered a contractual relationship with the deity, and distasteful. Kali guides him, even in the job he does not particularly like, but, he said, "She is moving me to do her will." He saw himself as her agent, a human being who simply had "blind faith in Kali," and relied on her mercy. If his modest, small home (as I saw) is what Kali wanted for him, so be it. If she had wanted him to live well, he would have. It was "enough" that when he called on her she was there—as she had been at critical times in his life. His wife was similarly free in her ritual activities, "sitting" in prayer after her bath but not meditating, she didn't know how to. Both were critical of the ostentatious show of devotion at Kalighat Temple, of people crying "so easily," and beating their heads on the stairs to the sanctum. Both were especially critical of the "occasional" devotees, the very rich who displayed their wealth and arrogance in large donations at the Temple.

EXPERIENCES RELATED TO FOOD
OFFERINGS AND FAMILY WELL-BEING

Sumona, a middle-aged woman whose husband Sachin we have met in chapter 4, had been drawn to the worship of Kali from her maternal side of the family: "We learned how worship is done," she said, "how to put vermilion on the deity, to offer the gods in our home food, water, and sweets, and arrange the flowers." I asked, how important is ritual worship to you? She replied, such acts draw her close to the deity, by repeatedly taking the trouble, as "habit," *abhyas*: "It's not easy to receive God. The images are made of stone, we know that. But there is life inside, a light." When I asked why she performed ritual, she replied, for her *man* to be at peace, but also because she simply loved to, and also "for those I love." [12]

Sumona recounted experiences in relation to food offerings, and to her family's well-being and health. She ate bhog at Kalighat Temple, because she "loves to," it "fills her *man*. . . . The sharing of food amongst my family is like sharing it with the Mother Kali when we ourselves eat it later." She had been initiated along with Sachin by their guru. Sumona commented, "Initiation purifies my atman . . . [one's] ties with the deity are closer. You want to cook for her." Sumona made special foods for the deities on her home altar, on festive occasions, whenever possible or when she could afford to, cooking mostly sweet foods, such as sweet coconut balls in thickened milk, rice pudding, and rice flour pancakes in syrup.[13] Sometimes she received "instructions in dreams," svapnades, where Kali would suggest a particular food that she wanted. She remembered (unusually among my participants) an approximate date for an event, which she then recounted. Sachin and she had been initiated at end-April, around 1968 or 1969. So she decided to offer bhog on Kali's annual festival at home that year and then again the following year, with curried lentils, vegetables, fruits and rice pudding. She recounted the following "event":

In the second year that we worshiped Kali in our home, as I was cooking bhog, two small dark children, a girl and a boy, came to my kitchen door and asked for a share. I told them, after the worship is done, you can have some. Go and sit in the room [with the altar]. I shut the kitchen door and went back to cooking, as the children left. After I was done, I brought the food in, and sat to worship at the altar, not noticing that the children were not there. I finished praying, and laid out the bhog in bowls. I then asked my Mother, "I cooked this for you, but how will I know that you have accepted my offering?" I was crying. Then I left the room. When I returned soon after, I saw with my own eyes that there was food on the image. The next day the two children showed up again. I was angry, and asked why they had not stayed on the day before. They said they had not come at all, and had not known I was celebrating Kali's festival.

She explained, "This is the Mother's 'play.' She answers my prayers in her own way."

Kali protects those Sumona loves. Her son had been failing in Class 9 when, as she wept, "someone" touched her, and "spoke in her *man*." The silent voice asked her to go to the school, and speak with the teachers. Sachin had refused to plead for his son. She did, and the boy then passed that grade. In another account, when one of her gold earrings fell into a pond, Sumona asked the goddess for its return, because she could not afford to make another one. A little boy got into the water, and picked up a leaf (everyone was searching)—the earring was on the leaf. Sumona observed: "This is the Mother's compassion. She has never hurt me." In yet another incident, her eldest daughter's child, then ten, was suddenly unable to walk or talk. Doctors at an American charitable hospital in Kolkata saw the girl but could not diagnose the problem. She would live, they said, but would be paralyzed. They suggested that the child be seen in the United States. But Sumona refused, because Kali appeared to her in a dream, and advised her against this step, suggesting that she make offerings at different temples. "Kali showed herself to the child," Sumona explained, to justify her decision, evidently a right one. "Twenty one days later," Sumona concluded, "She recovered, and uttered the word 'Ma.' A few days later she walked. It was the Mother who made her walk. The child is now well." Sumona said again, "The Mother shows herself in so many ways."

Sumona described "another time" when Sachin had stomach problems and it was feared he had tuberculosis. The Sakti goddess Kamakhya[14] appeared in a dream to him and said, "My tongue is dirty," and showed him her tongue. Next day, Sachin told Sumona, "Your grandmother showed me her tongue in a dream, and went away." Sumona went to her grandmother, and asked if she had come to see Sachin, but her grandmother had not: "Then I saw on her [grandmother's] altar, the goddess Kali's tongue as indeed being dirty. I wept, and vowed, 'I will give you gold eyes and tongue, and offer you worship." Sachin recovered. Sumona concluded: "Why then will I not say that the Mother is present?"

Sumona ended her stories with these reflections: "This is how I live [referring to her poverty]. But I live in peace. There are people poorer than us. We have time to pray, since my husband is not working. Kali is a stern mother. She makes her children suffer. We had a car once, and a house in [another part of Kolkata]. We have a phone now, and our daughters are well-settled.

Our son is spoiled by his father." Evidently, as I understood, these were luxuries afforded by her Mother Kali's compassion.

RITUAL DIFFERENCES WITHIN A
MARRIAGE, POSSIBLE EXPERIENCES

I spoke at length with Manju, Nandita's aunt-in-law, an attractive woman in her mid-thirties, at her well-appointed home in southern Kolkata. She was married to Deb, about forty, who ran a successful business in gold jewelry. Unlike Sumona, she claimed no "events" in her life, but would see her devotional proclivities as something instilled in her from her youth. Yet she spoke of flexibility in her ritual activities, choosing, for example, to not go to Kalighat Temple on Tuesdays and Saturdays, when the Temple was crowded, and, above all, the days on which animal sacrifices were performed in number. As the daughter-in-law of a privileged family, Manju was given special access to the Temple sanctum on festive days, and would go to offer flower garlands, and to pray. But on other days, she went only if she felt like it. However, she asserted that she was profoundly and expressly devout in her religious practices.

Manju described herself as "always" religious:

My paternal grandmother, paternal aunt, and my mother, I saw them all in a devotional light from when I was little. Our gurudev would come to our house, as would other holy men. We would sing devotional songs, perform rituals. My paternal aunt, who had been widowed at a young age, would, before we left for school, make us pray to Siva. She would have us, as a routine duty, arrange the flowers and leaves[15] for worship, and teach us how to make sandalwood paste. So, from when I was very young these things were inside me.

She described her faith in the Mother Kali as "huge" and professed a love for the deity from an early age. She attributed this early attraction to a temple that stood across from her childhood home. Every evening the rites of adoration were performed at this temple, as were the goddess Durga's annual festival rites in October. Manju noted that her devotional proclivities had increased as she had grown older. She walked to Kalighat Temple when she could: "If I am unable to go, my *man* is disturbed. If I leave Kolkata, I feel restless. This is the Mother's compassion. If she didn't have this mercy,[16] I would not feel this 'connection' with her."[17]

She was especially proud of founding Mangalik, in 1981 (with Nandita), comprised of a group of women who met weekly, and on festive occasions sang devotional songs. Mangalik also did charitable work such as distributing

food to the poor during the goddess Durga's festival. Mangalik was an espe-
cial expression of her devotion. Its weekly performances were, she said,
drawing larger crowds; holy men came to speak on special days, for example,
Ramakrishna's birthday—a saint for whom she felt great devotion. Her own
role in Mangalik involved arranging flowers for performances on auspicious
days, like Kali's annual festival. She would go to Kalighat Temple, purchase
a "fat garland" of red hibiscus for the altar at home, and let it bloom for the
event.

Manju related her good fortune, both from a devotional as well as from a
familial point of view to possible good deeds in an earlier life: "My mother-
in-law and my father are guru brother and sister,' *guru bhai bon*, both had
been initiated by the same guru." So, she observed, there had been a continuity in the trajectory of her devotional life, a spiritual kinship, and passed
down a generation:

> In this life I spend so much time with religion, I must have been similarly-
> minded in a previous life, so God has made the necessary connections for me in
> this life. Suppose I had ended up with a family [of in-laws] who were not believ-
> ers. What would I have done? Most of all, I want peace. I don't have children. I
> stay with the Mother. I ask that my life be blessed, full of joy, ananda. Nothing
> else. For this I pray to her. I try to behave well with everyone, and with my
> gurudev's compassion, my in-laws all love me very much. And he too, who has
> seen me from when I was young, also loves me greatly. He initiated me after I
> married and came to my in-laws.

Manju claimed no experiences of a miraculous kind, but briefly mentioned that she had heard of such experiences related to their guru. However,
he did appear to her in dreams, which she describes as his gift of darsan.
But, she said, in answer to my question, "If I need something for worship, I
get it. See! All desires are fulfilled. The pure desires of the *man*, the Mother
fulfills these, without a doubt. . . . Just incense and devotion [is all that is
needed]."

However, on reflection, she recounted an incident two years prior, related
to her husband, Deb:

> My husband had gone out early in the morning near our neighborhood. He fell
> [on the street] and broke his knee cap. One of the boys from a shop nearby
> phoned me, saying, 'Didi [older sister], don't be afraid, Dada [older brother] fell
> on the road. He is conscious, but his leg is probably broken, we are taking him to
> the hospital.' I went to see him. I was very nervous. He needed surgery. Because
> of Ma Kali's compassion, we met some really good doctors at the nursing home.
> In my being, and with every breath, I called on our goddess [here Jagaddhatri,

her in-laws' deity].[18] I called on our guru, as I sat in the nursing home's garden, and meditated with the mantra given to me by him. Of course, there is no difference between Kali, Durga, and Jagaddhatri—though all are separated in pictures at our home altar, along with our guru's picture. All of them are one in him. During that incident I felt my faith powerfully. I called on God, fed my husband caranamrta from the Temple and from our altar at home, and he recovered.

Everything, Manju observed, is a matter of the *man*. Her faith was reinforced by the books she read, whether the sayings of Ramakrishna in the *Kathamrta*, or those written by the "sons" of Ramakrishna's disciple Vivekananda. She had learned from the "insight"[19] of the authors. "I myself don't have a mother. I think of [the goddess] as real, as my own mother. . . . I believe that there is life in this image, Ma Kali will respond if called. If one calls with bhakti, the Mother will respond, this is my belief. Sometimes during crises, I think of Ma Kali, and I am safe. I think all this is her compassion."

Manju described her husband Deb's religious activities as less "outer," *bahhjik*, than hers, but observed: "His bhakti is great. . . . He believes deeply in our family's deity." Deb had chosen not to be initiated by his family's guru, who had initiated Manju. I asked Deb how he understood devotion and to describe his style of worship. He replied:

Before I get out of bed I remember God in my *man*, 10–15 minutes. . . . Before I leave for my morning walk I say the Gayatri mantra. My route is fixed. I think such and such between this much distance. Beltala, Hazra, Raja Basanta Roy Road, I have it measured. It takes me one and half hours . . . my *man* feels good.

When I ask if there is a deity that he particularly thinks of, as he walked, he replied:

No, I think of them all. I think of Ma Durga, Jagaddhatri, Kali, Tara, Sitala, and Annapurna, who are all in our house. Then I think of my maternal grandparents, paternal grandparents, my father, and then our guru. I pray for everyone's well-being. . . . I have to be with my deities, our guru, and my ancestors. . . . There are others who walk in groups, who discuss family matters. I have no sons, no next generation. So I like to walk alone. My *man* finds joy in this. In the morning my *man* is empty. So my walk is an easy one. I don't worry about my health, or material things. . . . My *man* tells me that for this I don't have to sit at our home altar. As Ramakrishna said, there is no particular place to call on God. I have no "place, time, objects" [*sthan kal patra*] for worship. I ask that I may walk on the right path, so that I don't fall out with people. I don't pray to get something.[20] I leave that to the deity. Depending on my bhakti I will get what I need. That person I want to meet, but have not been able to, may suddenly appear in front of me. This is "miraculous," alaukik. Then I realize that my prayer has reached God, and my *man* will be at rest. . . . I realize then that the deity has heard me and sent that person to me. I myself have nothing to do with this.

Deb described such experiences as a divine "progress report" [*sic*] on him:

I've cast my *man* at [the deity's] feet. She then makes me do things. I go wherever I need to and thank her for letting me get home safely. I have great bhakti. But I don't have outer show nor do I show off my devotion. I believe I will not get rewards if I do this.

Deb, like Manju, preferred to avoid Kalighat Temple on Tuesdays and Saturdays: "I have my own mother at home. My father's dead. If both parents were alive one would expend 50% on each. Here I expend one hundred percent on my mother. I wake in the morning and ask God, give me the opportunity to serve my [human] mother. Mother is the deity."

When I asked if Deb saw the goddess in his dreams, he replied:

Rarely. I do see my guru sometimes. I don't talk about these experiences . . . My "line" [*sic*] is such, I've thrown myself at Ma's feet, let her keep me as she thinks fit, keep me well, keep me unwell. My leg, for example, healed completely [from his fall]. From whom I receive, I keep my head bowed, I owe her. To whom I give, that gift is saved for me on the other shore. The fruits are there for me in my next life, perhaps not this one. So I keep trying.

He extended such "fruits" to his bhakti for his parents, and the "blessing," asirvad, they bestowed on him in return:

A human too is God, his blessing is great. Such blessing can't be purchased. The inside must be still to receive such blessing. I am the only son. . . . I've arrived here only with the blessing of my parents and my ancestors. My parents' suffering will make no one great . . . . My father left me this house. I have expanded it, because I like to keep his memory alive. The fact that I've been able to do all this, is his blessing, not my own ability. . . . Since I am doing well, I think that I am on the right path.

DEVOTION, CASUALLY

Ranu, a plump and attractive woman in her early forties, was the acting principal of a school for children with disabilities in southwestern Kolkata when I met her in her office. She described herself as a member of a family that was not too particular about its ritual practices. However, she would describe her work at the school as an act of devotion, bhakti, and share an account of an extreme ritual of sacrifice, the offering of blood from her own body to the goddess when her daughter had been very unwell. Her father, Ranu said, was a Kali devotee who carried a picture of Kali everywhere, and who would visit the Kali temple even when they had lived in Dehra Dun, in northwest India, across the country from Kolkata. She had been schooled at a Roman Catholic institution in Dehra Dun. When she accompanied her father to the Kali temple as a child, she would make the sign of the cross. (Her three daughters too were presently studying at Loreto Convent, an elite and expensive Roman Catholic school run by nuns in central Kolkata). However, she came to believe in Kali, even as a child, she said, when her ailing brother had recovered, after her father had offered worship at Kalighat Temple in Kolkata. At this time she came to see Kali as "alive and awake," jagrata, a protective mother who evidently would answer if called upon.

Ranu described her ritual activity as casual. She did perform Laksmi puja on Thursdays, and on full moon days, as prescribed for women. Her home altar included, besides the goddesses Laksmi and Kali, also images of the Buddha, and she intended to add one of Jesus shortly, she said. Her visits to Kalighat Temple were related to specific undertakings, such as before leaving for the United States to study for her master's degree in Human Development at Purdue University, and again after she returned. While at Purdue, not knowing the times of the full moon, she fasted on Thursdays, to the consternation of her friends (she noted).

Her husband too was not particularly devout, though he carried a picture of Kali with him. Her fifteen-year-old daughter made, in Ranu's words, some ritual motions to Kali at the home altar. Her other two daughters were "embarrassed" to take part in rituals. Implying that a cosmopolitan family had something to do with how she perceived the expression of bhakti, she told me that her brothers, while "ultra-modern," did, however, believe in Kali.

Ranu, when I asked, observed that she had not experienced anything miraculous in her life. However, upon reflection she recounted how, when her daughter had been unwell for a long time she had offered blood from her chest, along with a red hibiscus, vermilion, and milk sweets at Kalighat Temple. She had also given up eating sweets, as a personal sacrifice at this time, and described this as an act of devotion, bhakti. This had the "utmost effect" when the child recovered. Ranu showed me the half-inch scar on her upper chest from which she had offered blood.[21]

THE EXPERIENCE AS IMPETUS TO RITUAL

Where Deb looked on his material well-being as a blessing from his parents, benevolent ancestors, and the deity for his devotion, Ananda, like Abhijit, credited the goddess with resolving the great hardship he had encountered in life, and affording him the ability to see to his family in a time of trouble. He worked at an export firm, and had also played the Indian drums professionally. (We met Ananda earlier in this book.) He offered a history of how he became a devotee, beginning in childhood, and given impetus by remarkable events.

While his father had been an agnostic, Ananda said, his father's older brother was a devotee of Kali. When young, as he (Ananda) would go downstairs, he would smell the fragrance of incense from his uncle's worship room, and would stand with his head at the door. The stain from his forehead would remain on the door for many years. When he was about thirteen or fourteen years old (this was British India), he met a revolutionary and teacher named Pranab M. From him, Ananda learned about revolution, and would be arrested for his activities. His father went to the police station, and gave a signed guarantee that his son would no longer participate in such activities. Ananda was released, but suspended from school. He stayed home for a year, then entered a high school in southwest Kolkata, at which time he changed his name to Ananda from his previously given one. He graduated high school in 1949 (two years after Independence). Then in 1950 his father died. Till then, because his father had a good job they had "lived in happiness," but now the family fell on troubled times. At seventeen Ananda took over as head of the family. He had since, he said, seen to his responsibilities, arranging the marriage of his two brothers and two sisters. But this history served as preface and context for the events he then described.

Ananda broke his left hand in an accident, and could not work as a musician. The family's financial situation had been dire, and he had had to sell his mother's jewelry to make ends meet. About this time (1952) Pranab M. made another appearance in his life, and asked Ananda to accompany him at midnight to the Keoratala cremation grounds to meet a holy man. Ananda was a member of a charitable group which used to take the abandoned bodies of destitute people to Keoratala for cremation. He knew that the area was a meeting place for "anti-social elements," but, he said, he was not afraid to go there. He described what happened:

> At Keoratala it was very dark. From the blackness a voice called out my nickname.[22] I was frightened. My friend [Pranab] told me not to fear. I went up to the voice. The man, speaking in Hindi, told me various facts about myself, such as my father's death, the work I did, and addressed me by *tu*.[23] I thought he had learned all this from my friend, but Pranab told me he had not said anything to the holy man.[24] Anyway, this man advised me to chant the *Narayani stotra*,[25] beginning the next day, and then every day of my life. He said my life would not be easy, but I would prevail. I offered him salutations but did not touch him,

and my friend and I left. I never saw the man again. That he had some kind of spiritual ability I do not doubt.

My life indeed took a turn for the better after this event. I was in such a desperate situation, I did not know how to feed my family. I grasped at that holy man's advice. So it is that faith is born. As my troubles eased, I came to the firm belief that God does indeed show [herself] in our lives.

Ananda began practicing meditation by chanting the *Narayani* incantation, as advised by the mysterious holy man. But this would require effort. He would sit daily to visualize Kali's face and initially found it impossible, he said. Twenty-two years old at the time, all he could "see" were the faces of pretty young women. He asked himself if there were differences in "seeing," but would come to realize that "to see the deity, and to see oneself truthfully, and the changes in oneself as one progresses on the spiritual path, is difficult, though possible." He was the only one of all his siblings who reflected on such matters, including why the deity is simultaneously given form, but is also without form. Giving deity form made her accessible, devotion became easier, Ananda noted. But Sakti is without form, to understand this is the end-goal of the devotee. Ananda illustrated his reflections with another story from Ramakrishna's life. For the saint, he said, Kali laughed, and ate foods he offered to her. But when Ramakrishna died no one else saw such things. So, Ramakrishna's very devotion brought his clay deity to life, Sakti as palpably present.

Ananda elaborated on the ritual "requirements" such as a purifying bath before worship as acts of discipline that focused the *man*. With practice, this became easier, the *man* could be brought to stillness, in preparation for that which is "to be seen." He described such effort as "dressing as the goddess in one's *man*" embodying in himself those qualities of Kali lauded in the hymn. Where the icon of Kali (and her accoutrements) is also who she *is*, Ananda, in visual and in word aspired to be one with her: "We pray to our own sakti."

During meditation, on occasion, Ananda described the light he would see as "auspicious seeing," darsan:

> After I have succeeded in quieting my *man*, I see a light. I can't see this, however, until my outer organs [eyes, ears,] are closed. At first, this light moves, in two waves of gold and blue, with white at its center, flashing like lightning. As my *man* becomes more focused, the light becomes still. At this point, I have no sense of time. I can sit in meditation for three days and still feel that I have only begun. . . . We live in the middle. We don't know the beginning, or the end.

Again, Ananda referred to Ramakrishna's experience. After a long period of meditation, the saint demands to know why Kali will not show him her "true" formless self. She appears to him, and demands that he sever her clay image with her "sword of knowledge." As he does so, at the moment of severance, the saint finds himself in a sea of light, where light and darkness are indistinguishable.[26]

Ananda's devotional experiences led to crossing social and religious boundaries. Declaring his impatience with social discrimination, he invited a Muslim and his family to his sister's wedding (he had borrowed money from this man). The Brahman caretakers at Kalighat Temple, also guests, refused to eat with Muslims. Then his friend, the musician Santosh, also a Brahman, and his brother (a caretaker at the Temple) sat down to eat. Once the Brahmans sat to eat, so did the other guests. People said that this "impurity" would bring inauspiciousness (as "calamity," amangal) on Ananda's family, and on his sister. However, Ananda concluded, she was fine. On another occasion and after he had had tea at Alokebabu's temple, Ananda wiped his (now ritually polluted) hand on his head, and, in a deliberate act, put a fallen flower back on image of the deity. Alokebabu looked at him and asked why he had done this. Ananda responded: "If a child puts his unclean hand on his mother will she cast him out?" Alokebabu had agreed.

FROM RELIGIOSITY TO ATHEISM

Bimala's journey takes a different turn, from high religiosity to atheism. This was especially surprising to me, as I had attended the celebration of Kali's annual festival at her mother's home during my first phase of research. Bimala expressly and briskly declared her impatience with the miraculous. A plump, lively woman of around fifty, Bimala lived with her husband and son in an apartment in a high-rise in south-western Kolkata. I would come to know her well, eventually as a friend with whom I spent time talking about my research interests, and about my family in the United States. She would comment early on that till I showed up she had never stopped to ask the "why" behind her rituals, which she performed daily, and assiduously. Her home altar included a diversity of deities, different versions of Krsna, both Daksina Kali and Kali as Adyama, Siva, an aninconic Laksmi (in the form of a jar, *ghat*), Ramakrishna, the Krsna saint Caitanya, the Buddha, and Sri Aurobindo (1872–1950).[27]

Bimala's religious activities were many when I first met her: she went to Kalighat Temple in time for the ritual awakening of Kali, managalarati, at 5 a.m. She performed special rites for the goddess Laksmi at home on Thursdays. She declared with a laugh that she was seeing to it that "everyone," that is, all the divinities would be there to call on, as individual insurance policies depending on the exigency.

Bimala declared frankly that her devotion was inspired by fear, but she could deviate from ritual rigidity. Here she cited Ramakrishna as "authorizing" the freedom of a devotee to express her devotion as she chose. So she participated in the cooking of bhog at the annual festival of the goddess Durga at the high rise, and at Kali's annual festival at her mother's home, simply because she "loved to." She had made the choice to not to be initiated by a guru, and, she said, she hoped her devotion would cancel out any ritual failing on her part.

Bimala would be the only woman among my participants who expressed feminist views (though she had never heard of this political concept, and I did not make a point of it). So, she said, even as a Brahman woman, she was discriminated against, and could not utter certain mantras even though an uneducated Brahman cook could do so, simply being a man—despite his lower social class. This, despite the fact that her maternal family was learned in the texts, she said. Why are women, she asked, not permitted to perform public worship at the goddess' festivals or at temples? If women were fasting for their husbands and children, who were fasting for the women? (I did not comment on her critique of patriarchy)! She would add that women are defined only by their relationships, as wife, mother, and sister, and were held back in their lives.

However, much would change in Bimala's religious views and practices. The cause of the tragedy that befell her at the high-rise would be attributed to a fire, and interpreted as the "cause" of her personal tragedy. On the final day of worship at the Durga festival (Dashami), at which I was present, married women of the community, bidding the goddess farewell, went up to the six-feet high clay image one at a time, holding brass plates with containers of vermilion and a lit oil lamp. The vermilion is applied to the face and forehead of the deity, while the lamp is waved in circular movements in front of the image—in this context, simultaneously an act of adoration, and farewell for another year. One of the women brought her lamp too close to the by-now-dry, five-day-old garlands that adorned the image. I had my camera pointed at this emotional ceremony, and was the first to see, through the lens, a huge flame shoot up in the confined space of the parking lot of the high-rise, consuming the deity's garlands and sari in a moment. I shouted, "Fire!" as several young men in the watching crowd sprang into action, dousing the image with buckets of water.

In the noisy activity that ensued, one of the priests present commented quietly to me that devotion is all very well, but common sense is also called for! A young man reached up to the clay face of the goddess, now inauspiciously black with soot, and cleaned it. I, taller than many of the women present, assisted. A new red sari was brought, and draped around the deity, as conch shells sounded to ward off malign presences drawn by the inauspicious event.

I would learn that such carelessness, seen as injury to one's "daughter," here the goddess Durga, could result in the deity's wrath, at some *dosa*, or inherent "moral fault" in the community of the high-rise.

Such wrath, read in retrospect in events to come, would find proof. On New Year's Eve that year (1986), as Bimala and her husband celebrated at a party, he fell dead of a heart attack. But earlier the same year, in August, a young woman in this high-rise had suddenly died. This sudden death had stunned the mostly middle-class professionals, and retired and elderly people living in the high rise. After Bimala's husband's untimely death, divine displeasure, it was felt in consensus, required placating and penance. In February the following year Santi Puja, the "rite for peace," was performed by a priest at the high rise to the aniconic version of the goddess, a jar containing water from the Ganga, and leaves of the mango tree. After the worship, sanctified water from the jar was sprinkled on the door of all forty apartments by the priest, in an act of ritual cleansing and penance.

I found that Bimala had undergone a seismic shift in sensibilities. She told me that she had wrapped the many gods on her altar in a blanket, and rolled them under her bed. She was now, she said, reading books denying the presence of God. The gods had not delivered, as she had hoped and prayed, these many years. She owed them nothing. Bimala would staunchly maintain her atheistic stance in the years I would meet her, in 1992 when I returned on a post-doctoral grant, and for the last time in 2010.

The eight people whose stories I present in this chapter speak to differences in life circumstances and trajectories, in socio-economic circumstances, choices of religious practice, and experiences—and differences in understanding what such experiences mean. However, they also speak to culturally shared concepts, and their practices and experiences find context in such sharing. Bhakti, centrally, is about devotion to, and connection with the deity. Such feeling maybe "inside" oneself, from youth, instilled by family tradition, but also practiced, nurtured and strengthened over time. Bhakti is both practice, and journey, "outer" and "inner," one of ritual practices involving Temple visits, rites of adoration, song—or meditation, or both. Bhakti is expressly social, a moral and ethical connection extended to family, and applied to one's elders and to a preceptor, for both female and male devotees. Such connection, even in Bhakti's root meaning, that of incorporation, devotee in deity, is by definition reciprocal, albeit hierarchical. Disinterested bhakti yields, in Deb's words, "fruits," even when unsought. Ranu speaks of her dedicated work for the less fortunate at the school for children with disabilities as bhakti. Devotion can be to the abstract and formless divinity, as Sakti, and to the iconic one; or both, where such apparent dualities are in fact, one. The home altars of the devotees, including the "chosen deity," the goddess Jagaddhatri in Deb's family, are inclusive, even of gurus, philosopher saints like Sri Aurobindo, and Jesus. As on Alokebabu's temple wall, the deities and humans are an eclectic collection; devotion to one is devotion to all, even if one may be preferred. Devotees choose that journey, one that requires effort and perseverance. Bhakti is sacrifice, giving up sweets so a daughter will heal, lending additional power to the "gift" of blood from her chest, for Ranu. It is a prayer on a daily morning's walk, or a daily visit to the Temple, over decades, to offer salutations to the goddess, for Abhijit. Bhakti, variously, yields "fruits," removing obstacles, whether these be financial troubles, passing an exam, or getting a job. Bimala, an ardent devotee when I first met her, is the one voice of dissidence in these accounts, an outlier, where her bhakti is a transactional relationship with the deity, dispensed with when her bhakti does not yield the "fruits" she wants, the well-being of her husband.

Kali is anthropomorphic shape given to a divine, invisible, pervasive power, Sakti, another and central theme that runs through the narratives. Such power is unbounded, and unconstrained, and "plays" in astonishing ways, and by will—which devotees interpret, with wonder, but can't explain—but interpret as Sakti and as a compassionate, protective mother, Kali, who knows her devotee's *man*. Sakti is not external to the devotee. This power allows for remarkable incidents in Nandita's family of devotees, crossing boundaries of time and space. Sakti directs human agents, such as the "dark" children who appear, disappear, and then appear again in Sumona's story, "finds" her lost gold earring, and heals her grandchild, who utters her first word, "Mother," when she speaks again. Ananda, after his meeting with the mysterious holy man at the cremation grounds, takes his advice to chant a hymn glorifying the goddess, finds himself back on his financial feet, and is able to pay for the weddings of his siblings. The miraculous is understood across a spectrum in how it is expressed and communicated, but interpreted, evidently, as divine compassion, a Mother's love and protection in life's many exigencies, albeit in unpredictable ways. Such experiences suggest simultaneously that divinity is both real—and true. Why, asks Sumona, will she then not say that the Mother is there?

By the same token, where Sakti is a moral force (the mother Kali who can and should be stern), an event like a fire which causes damage (injury?) to the anthropomorphic image of the deity at her festival "explains" untimely deaths, such as Bimala's loss, as possible moral failing, dosa, in the high rise community. This needs rectifying, with worship and penance, in rites of peace, where the entire community is drawn in, and cleansed. In sum, transformations, in the person of a devotee, in his or her life circumstances, in actions he or she chooses to take but above all in the enhanced awareness in intimations of how Kali/Sakti works, as revealed in "experiences," anubhuti, offer a central and underlying theme to the accounts I recount above.

I explore in the next chapter the concept of moral failing in the concepts of "calamity" (amangal) as well as "auspiciousness and well-being" (mangal), in the context of sacrificial "gift offerings," balidan, to the Sakti goddess. This rite, central to her rituals of worship, would yield many accounts of experiences by devotees.

NOTES

1. From my personal collection of his music.
2. See Inden and Nicholas (1977); Mookerjee and Khanna (1977, 126); Ostor, "Red is the color of the goddess; vermilion is her favorite, symbolizing auspiciousness, victory, joy, and blood in sacrifice (1980, 69); see also Samanta (1992b).
3. The word *mangal*, says Eck, "reminds us that there is no Sanskrit term which quite corresponds to what we [of the West] mean by "sacred" (1981, 3, Fn 1).
4. Latin *clitoria*; *Aparajita* is an epithet for the goddess in the *Devi-Mahatmya* where the gods address her as the "Undefeated" to invoke her powers against the demons (5.8–82).
5. My translation from Bengali (from recorded music). See Hawley on poetry as the "natural vehicle" of bhakti, and the "galaxy of bhakti poets who have been moved to song" (2015, 2)
6. The ritual of awakening the goddess in the morning, with prayer, incense, offerings of food, water, and vermilion, and a symbolic bath.
7. Nandita uses the word anubhav, "experience," "empathy."
8. Nandita would know this about a stranger because she was not wearing the signs of marriage, such as vermilion in the part of her hair.
9. Nandita uses the word anubhav again.
10. See the "eternal guru" discussed in chapter 4.
11. Nandita uses the word "*tej*" here, which can mean "light," also "force" and "energy."
12. Sumona did in fact distinguish her style of worship from Sachin's, telling me that she "wandered around from temple to temple," while he preferred to stay home and meditate.
13. These sweets are labor-intensive to prepare, which is the point!
14. Kamakhya Temple is one of fifty-one holy sites across north India. Located in Assam state in northeast India, Kamakhya is the site where in myth the goddess Sati's genitalia fell to earth after her body was severed by the god Visnu's discus. This site is seen as especially *jagrata*, alive, and potent.
15. The leaves of the wood apple (*bel*) tree, special to the god Siva.
16. Manju uses the Bengali words *krpa*, *daya*, for both compassion and mercy.
17. Here Manju uses the word "pull," tan.
18. See McDermott on Jagaddhatri as another form of the goddess Durga (2009, 202).
19. Manju uses the word anubhav.
20. Deb uses the word *phal*, "fruits."
21. This is one type of sacrificial offering, atmabali, which I discuss in chapter 8.

22. This is reserved generally only for family, and close friends.

23. The second person imperative, *tui* (in Bengali) or *tu* (in Hindi) is used for close relationships, between friends, or by an elder addressing a younger person, or a social inferior like a servant. Both are gender-neutral terms. Kali may be invoked by *tui* (in song, for example) to express the intimate relationship the devotee has with her.

24. However, Ananda does tell me that Pranab M., with whom he had kept in touch over the years, had known about his financial troubles. So, it is possible that Pranab had indeed told the holy man about Ananda.

25. A hymn in in praise of the goddess, where she is invoked as earth, water, time, mother, protector and refuge, the Great Illusion (Mahamaya), slayer of demons, the "effulgent one," the embodiment of humility, respect, intelligence, wisdom, wrathful, and destructive of desire (Jagadarisvananda, *Devi-Mahatmya*, 11, 1–55).

26. Svami Sharadananda offers a description of Ramakrishna's famous experience of being engulfed in an ocean of light when he attempts to see beyond dualities (1956). See chapter 1 earlier, Romain Rolland on Ramakrishna's "oceanic feeling," 1927).

27. Sri Aurobindo was a philosopher, poet, and nationalist, who founded the Sri Aurobindo Asram in the southern Indian territory of Pondicherry.

Chapter 8

Sacrificial Offering to Kali, Experiences of Well-being and Calamity

The penultimate act, just prior to the offering into fire (homa) in the sequential progression of Kali's rituals at temples, or at her annual rites, is one of animal or vegetable sacrifice as "gift offering," balidan.[1] Bali draws from the Sanskrit root *bhr*, meaning to support, protect, and maintain—the moral order of the universe. Sacrificial offerings of animals and/or vegetables are textually prescribed, and mandatory in Kali's worship and for other Sakti goddesses. Several discourses, in legend, myth, and scripture emphasize the powerful efficacy of bali, and variously comment on this ritual.[2]

Accounts of experiences related to balidan were interpreted by participants in terms of the concepts of "well-being," mangal, and "calamity," amangal. Balidan was, as I describe later, emotionally intense, and for good reason. Present as well as future "well-being" for an individual, his immediate family, and even his extended patriline depend crucially on the success or otherwise of this rite. Where the fluid concept of Sakti lies in a relationship between deity and the sacrifier,[3] divinity is not "other" and separate from him but in a potentially transformable relationship.[4] In exegetical commentary, ritual and myth, the self of the sacrifier is equated with the "animal" (pasu), and the "animal's" transformation is effected within a metaphor of divine ingestion and digestion.[5] Appropriately, a "failed" bali, where the animal is not killed with one stroke of the sword, is described as "obstructed," presaging "calamity" in this life, and possibly in future ones. The converse holds true, in the case of a "successful" offering. As the devourer of demons in myth,[6] or as the protective Mother-goddess in Bhakti belief, Kali is transcendent of uncontrolled sexuality. Appropriately, the goat represents lust, one of "six enemies," *sararipu*.[7] The sacrificial animal is thus a gift of the animal-like sacrifier, who is limited in what he can perceive, but has the potential to be transformed.[8]

Balidan's efficacy, ideally resulting in his own "well-being" and that of his loved ones, is related to the purity of the sacrifier's *man*. He offers himself in "surrender," *utsarga kara*. This is followed by a verbal "declaration of intent" *sankalpa*. This declaration locates the social person in Time by astrological configuration, and by name, caste, and the larger social group, his *gotra* affiliation.[9] Such transformation, then, is both understood and aspired to at a cosmic level, and "obstruction" is not an option. Much is at stake, and offers context to the emotional intensity I observed when the rite was performed, and to the accounts I would hear from participants.

Bali, as animal sacrifice, continues to be performed in vast numbers, as I myself saw it.[10] On Kali's annual festival some 700 or more goats may be offered, many "vow"-related, *manater bali*, in return for a loved one to recover from illness. On Tuesdays and Saturdays, days auspicious to Kali, seventy animals may be offered on each day. At Kalighat Temple a daily sacrifice of a single goat is commissioned by the caretakers. The meat of the animal is later cooked and offered to the deity as part of her daily food offering, as bhog. Portions of this are subsequently purchased and consumed by worshipers as divine grace, prasad. The rite involves the purchase of a healthy, young, and unblemished black male goat, by prescription in the ritual manual, *SriSri Kalipuja Paddhati*. The animal's head is fixed between the prongs of a forked cast iron post about three feet high and set in concrete

Figure 8.1   Site of Sacrifice, Balidan, at Kalighat Temple, Kolkata. *Source*: Photograph by the author.

(see Figure 8.1), due south of the goddess' sanctum in the temple. Once red hibiscus and vermilion have been offered to the animal, to the post, and to the sword, and deities have been invoked, the sacrificer severs, at one stroke, the goat's head from its body.

I witnessed the ritual of goat sacrifice at Kalighat Temple, and gourd sacrifice on Kali's annual festival at Bimala's mother's home (see Figure 8.2). "Self-sacrifice," which involves the offering of blood from one's own body, was shared with me by Ranu, at the school for children with disabilities (see chapter 7). I would hear about "sacrifice to foxes" (*Sivabalidan*) from a male participant. I personally saw how critical this rite was at the Temple, and at Bimala's home, as worshipers seemed to hold their breath until the severance (for both animal and gourd) was indeed a clean one.

I would observe that emotional intensity in balidan at Kalighat Temple. The excerpt below is from my journal notes:

> The official sacrificer of Kalighat Temple . . . and another man . . . carried the goat, struggling and bleating pathetically, to the sacrificial post. Its head was secured with a horizontal iron rod penetrating the two prongs of the forked cast iron post, while its four legs were held stretched at its back by the second man. The sacrificer then positioned himself on the right side of the goat and touched the neck of the animal with his sword.

Figure 8.2 Gourd Sacrifice, on Kali's Annual Festival at Devotee's Home. *Source:* Photograph by the author.

Meanwhile a crowd had gathered around the square. As the sacrificer lifted his curved sword, it remained poised for what seemed like a timeless moment. I experienced what was for me the most powerful point of any of the rituals of the goddess. My feelings were evidently shared by my fellow observers, for they too, it seemed, held their breath. . . . I have very little recollection of that moment, before the sword fell. It seemed [that] . . . far more than the violent and bloody death of an animal was at stake, where something central and crucial was being effected within the conceptual world of the Sakti goddess . . . the power of the moment and the tension and fear of the observers . . . implied that something momentous hung in the balance.

The sword fell, severing the goat's head cleanly from its body, releasing the observers' tension.

My notes continue with what followed, namely the removal of the animal and its severed head. The sacrificer smeared the blood (which had collected in a bowl placed between the prongs of the post) on the forehead of his assistant. The post was then washed with coconut water, and a mixture of this and blood, as the "nectar of immortality" was offered to worshipers, to touch to their lips. One young man, offering his salutations at the post, told me that his prayers here were equivalent to praying to the goddess herself in the Temple sanctum, and most efficacious in attaining one's desires—in his case, a job.

INDIVIDUAL RESPONSIBILITY FOR COMMUNITY "WELL-BEING"

The collective nature and moral implications of well-being and calamity is illustrated in this account of Sivabalidan, bali to jackals, the animal associated with Kali. I met Barun at his spacious home in south Kolkata. Claiming his antecedents as a princely family, he had worked for some time as a journalist and had lectured in the United States on the Indo-Chinese war of 1962 and the Bangladesh war of 1971. He was now a businessman working in collaboration with a Japanese firm which manufactured optical glass. His family had built a temple to Kali on his country estate, which he visited, and where goats were sacrificed on the goddess' annual festival. He recounted this experience:

I had returned [to my country estate] during Kali's annual festival and according to my family's tradition, the heads of goats were offered for jackals, at the borders of the forest adjoining our property. On one such occasion, no jackals appeared. The worshipers present, many thousands, some of whom were our tenants, took this for a certain sign of the calamity to come. In fact, they blamed me for this. In the face of an increasingly unpleasant crowd, I prayed to Kali with all my might, for two hours, before the jackals finally showed up and took the goat-heads away.

The contemporary "prince" and journalist commented to me skeptically that perhaps the jackals had not shown up because of the crowds. However, he was relieved that they did, for his own sake and that of his tenants.

ATMABALI, OFFERING OF THE SELF, AND *MANATER BALI*, VOW-RELATED OFFERING

Balidan is made as a "vow," *manat*, a promise of a "gift" to Kali should she resolve a problem in the sacrifier's life. These involve a promise privately made between worshiper and the goddess. Such bali may involve the sacrifice of a goat, or as atmabali, blood from the sacrifer's body (the right arm, or near the heart). Both types may be offered at times of crisis, outside of but also on festive occasions. Ranu, (in chapter 7), had made such a vow, of atmabali, to supplicate the goddess to heal her ailing daughter.

A guru can pierce his arm or chest, mix the blood with vermilion and with the appropriate declaration of intent on behalf of a beloved disciple, offer the items into the sacrificial fire, or in a bowl at the base of the goddess' image. The goddess "consumes" this offering after the guru utters the words, "Ma Kali, may [name of disciple] experience 'well-being,' mangal." It is believed that the guru takes upon himself the risks of failure, risking even his own life.[11]

The removal of transgression-as-illness may be achieved through balidan. A male devotee described the goddess' command in an auditory experience:

> At our country home during the annual festival for Kali many years ago, a small boy, aged five, suddenly fell very ill. The boy's father was a great devotee. He was busy with the worship, and did not go to see his son. He believed that Kali would come to his son's aid. His brother-in-law called him out in the early hours of the morning and asked him to get a goat for a "vow-related" offering, saying he had heard a voice saying, "I am taking away the disease-animal. There is no need to fear." The little boy recovered. We offered an animal as a vow honored. This is a "true event," satya ghatana.

CALAMITY RELATED TO PERSONAL MORALITY

The notion of moral responsibility in a failed balidan can be explicit, or implicit. Sometimes an "obstructed" sacrifice is directly attributed to the moral failing of the person who commissions the offering, the sacrifier. At other times these transgressions are not evident to him or her but become so in the outcome of the rite, suggesting some inherent fault in the person or misdeed in a past life of which he is obviously unaware. The following account by Santosh, who used to tutor a princely family in music and whom we have met earlier, illustrates this ambiguity in an account related to the observance of the goddess' annual festival at the prince's mansion. The prince, Santosh said, indulged in "excesses" such as sex with prostitutes, who were "specially" included in the celebrations, and continued:

> The feasting was excessive, and huge numbers of animals (goats, buffalo, and rams) exceeding 250 in number, were offered on Nabami [the auspicious ninth day of worship for the Sakti goddess Durga].[12] I warned the prince about his sexual transgressions. In 1971, seven years or so after I had taken up my duties with the prince, the goat being offered as bali got "stuck," and the head was severed from the body only by a second stroke of the sword. I prophesied to the prince that there were limits to his profligacy and that this would be the last festival for him. Next year, in 1972, on the second day of the festival [Saptami] the prince went for a hunt, returned, and right after the ceremony of welcoming the goddess, died suddenly of a heart attack. The festivities were ended.

The anecdotes associating an "obstructed" sacrifice to "calamity," amangal, were many. Bimala told me how on the annual festival of Kali a goat had been "stuck" and her brother-in-law had then suddenly died. The following year, another close female relative died, as a "consequence" of another such "obstructed" balidan. These incidents resulted in her family's decision to offer only vegetable sacrifices in future (this is what I myself observed at her home on Kali's festival). However, here too disaster struck. Of the five plants of sugarcane which are to be severed at once, one slipped the sacrifier's sword and flew out. Her young niece died soon after.

Tarun, one of the men who visited Alokebabu's temple and a businessman, offered several anecdotes related to the consequences, for better and worse, of balidan. His grandfather, who had been childless, had a son soon after offering bali. But, his two paternal uncles suffered the consequences of an "obstructed" bali, and gambled and squandered away the family wealth. Who knows why? Tarun asked, after relating these anecdotes. He remembered a story he had heard from Alokebabu, of a wealthy family whose bali had been "obstructed." This was followed, he said, by fraternal fights, a brother's suicide, and insanity in the family.

Tarun also described an event about a Tantric adept with whom he had a close relationship. This man, whom he called "father" (Baba), "had powers." The Tantric called Tarun's wife and sister "daughter," and Tarun himself his "son-in-law." This man worshiped Kali, and would begin by putting a flower on the image. He would then swear, weep, and plead with goddess. If the flower fell, it was a sign of the goddess having accepted his offering. When it did fall, said Tarun, it seemed as if it had been flung down. One time Tarun would witness the Tantric's powers in action at his oldest maternal uncle's home. The bali offered was that of a species of catfish, on a brick placed on an altar of sand. The fish were leaping about, when the Tantric called out loudly.[13] The fish froze (and, I assume, died). "There are some things," reflected Tarun, "which if one does not see for oneself, one cannot believe."

Balidan and experiences related to it are interesting in that mangal and amangal, well-being and calamity, are both interpreted, but are also amenable to explanation. Such explanation, unlike experiences described as anubhuti, offers a possible connection between cause and effect. Bali and its consequences find a coherent theme in a paradigm that traverses different discourses—in philosophical exegesis, in myth, in ritual, and in devotees' accounts of their experiences. In philosophical discourse a bestial animal-self is transformed in the act of offering itself to divinity. In myth, the demon (by definition an animal) is defeated in battle by Kali, and his head is offered to the goddess Durga as proof of conquest. The severed demon-head in Kali's left lower hand symbolizes the death of arrogance and the egotistical self, effected by the "sword of knowledge" which she wields. Purity of intent is required in the declaration of intent, made by the sacrifier before the ritual of offering as balidan. The forked cast iron pillar at the site for sacrifice at Kalighat Temple goes deep into concrete. As Mount Meru, where the gods reside, it is the fifth and vertical dimension of space and time, which must not shake. It is the moral center of the universe. Much then hangs in balance especially of animal and vegetable sacrificial offering to the Sakti goddess. Consequent "calamity" for the sacrifier's family (even down generations) is "explicable" by the sacrifier's moral failing in this life or in previous ones if the rite of offering is "obstructed" in an "unclean" killing. If Barun's account about the jackals taking their time to get the heads of sacrificed goats suggests concern at possible future calamity (because of his own failings), Santosh's account of the profligate prince's untimely death makes a direct connection between failed sacrifice and divine punishment. As I describe in my own observations, there is real fear among participants whether or not there will be a clean severance, of animal or vegetable. The converse holds true, evident by the immediacy of a disease healed, or simply a hoped-for well-being in the sacrifier's life, a child born to the childless, or a job, where this is sought. In the stories that speak to lived experience, there are accounts of those whose extreme self-offering, as atmabali, results in the restored health of a child, and of the powers of men who can still a leaping fish, offered in sacrifice, by a shout. Even as balidan can be, and is, often transactional, effecting changes in the present, the larger context of the rite's meaning within concepts of "well-being," mangal, and "calamity," amangal, suggest cosmic change, for better or worse. Experiences related to balidan are fraught and emotionally powerful for those commissioning the rite.

NOTES

1. I discuss the philosophical meanings of balidan in my paper (Samanta 1994). This chapter focuses on participants' experiences related to this rite.

2. Swami Jagadiswarananda (1985), *Devi Mahatmya*, 12. 10–11, 13; Pandit Srinityanananda Smrtitirtha (1981), *Kalitantram* 3); Dutt (1979), *Mahanirvana Tantram* 6.105); Blaquiere (1979), *Rudhiradhyaya* of the *Kalika Purana*, 371–373, 379.

3. Hubert and Mauss (1964) distinguish as "sacrificer" the man who actually performs the act, while "sacrifier" is the person who commissions the sacrifice, and to whom the benefits of sacrifice accrue. At Kalighat Temple, traditionally, a man of the low-ranked Bagdi caste serves as the sacrificer.

4. Das (1983) and Hayley (1980), writing on sacrifice in the Hindu context have criticized the theistic premise of interpretations of this rite in other cultural and religious contexts, where man and god are separate entities. Hayley notes the fluidity between concepts of god and devotee expressed in acts of offering, while Das emphasizes that it is the act itself, the centrality of the sacrifier's *intent* that lies at the heart of the rite of sacrificial offering in a Hindu belief. It is thus, he who is transformed.

5. Food and its processing is a theme that is found in Ayurvedic beliefs, where, for example, food is transformed to blood marrow, then to blood, and finally to semen, the source of progeny (Inden & Nicholas 1977). Absorbed nutrients become the human mind, undigested food becomes feces (Khare 1976). Food has moral qualities, and embodies those of the cook/offerer (Marriott 1976). A person is not only what he eats, but participates in the transformation of what he eats.

6. In the *Devi-Mahatmya* Kali offers demons she has killed to the goddess Durga (7.23–24).

7. The other five "enemies" are those of anger, greed, delusion, egotism, and envy, each represented by an animal.

8. Kaviraj, writing on Tantra philosophy, notes the cooking of the pasu/jiva as *dagdha*, "burnt" (1963). Sinha uses the same term to describe the "burning" of delusion by "immediate knowledge of Siva-Sakti" (1966, 9–10). The process of spiritual refinement, over eons, is expressed, thus, in a metaphor of progressive distillation of the "self-animal" as it is "cooked," toward ultimate enlightenment. Kali, Time, is the great devourer, in whose bowels the "self" is cooked. (See also Samanta 1994).

9. *Gotra* is an exogamous social group, analogous with "clan," where a mythical sage is the ancestor of the group. It is a different category of identification for a Hindu, and includes the endogamous identity of caste (*jati*). For a woman, her paternal gotra identity changes to that of her husband's family's gotra after marriage.

10. Foulston & Abbott observe that Kalighat is the largest urban temple where bali continues (2009, 198).

11. Babb describes the Radhasoami guru who looks at his disciples, and thereby "digests," transforms, and distills their "karmic residues" (1986, 211).

12. At Durga's annual festival (officially from the sixth to tenth day of the waxing moon in October-November), she is welcomed by worshipers on the seventh (Saptami). On the ninth day she defeated the demons in battle, and sacrifices are offered. The tenth day is celebrated as the "Day of Victory" (*Bijoya Dasami*).

13. A *humkar*, a particularly loud call, not accurately translatable into English.

Conclusion

I set out at the start of my research project to attempt an understanding of Bengali perceptions of Kali, an "inner" way of knowing and expression that might complement other approaches brought to interpretations of this complex deity by scholars in the West. I would find, as I have said, and to my surprise, an outpouring not of exegetical comment but of accounts of experiences that Kali's devotees evidently felt best answered my question. Businessmen, clerical workers, musicians, women at home and at work, and others, going about their everyday lives, expressed their perception of the goddess in terms of what I have called alaukik ghatana, "miraculous events," across a spectrum of such experiences. None of my participants, while calling themselves devotees (bhaktas) of Kali, claimed the status of a mystic—including Alokebabu, irrespective of others' perceptions of his powers. In their recollections of experiences they described an ongoing and spiritual journey, sometimes implicitly, a process of change, of becoming. They interpreted rather than explained their experiences in a context of cultural understanding, suggesting other ways of knowing, in a tradition where this evidently continues to be not only possible but also accepted and valid. I end by reiterating the insights that the "father of Kali studies," David Kinsley, had to offer, that "one must seek to discern the visionary aspect of a religious phenomenon, one that legitimates it as a religious thing," to be "open to possibilities beyond the ordinary," where "something other" suggests that which is "ultimately meaningful" (1975a, 4).

Kali's devotees described or inferred in their accounts of experiences of Kali or of their guru the transformations effected in themselves by a malleable and fluid force, Sakti. These experiences, as "intuitive insights," anubhuti, recollected and reflected upon in the *man* were integral to such change, where meaning was found in the *process* of remembrance. Ultimately, the "play" of the eternal Sakti, in lights, dreams and human manifestations, *is*

119

in a relationship, and transformation is effected in the person, hence Dinu's comment that he had seen his true "self," atman.

Anubhuti, as experiential "knowing" and as impetus toward moral and spiritual transformation may be understood at two levels. Such experiences are described as being "real events" asal ghatana, as well as "true events," satya ghatana, though these are loosely bounded, and perhaps understandably so. The "real" aspect of experiences have a material reality in the physical world of cause and effect. They involve, by extraordinary means—interpreted as the "play" of Kali/Sakti or the guru's sakti—the actual fruition of predictions in dreams, and the resolutions of crises in the real world. Experiences also involve the unusual movements of humans in a sequence of related events in perceptible time and space while also being transcendent of these dimensions. So, Sachin's guru describes his own experience, and how this led to his renunciation of a career in medicine to pursue the spiritual path. Nandita tells me the extraordinary story of the young woman who comes at some unknown bidding to the family's temple and completes the ritual of offering vermilion to Kali. In her second account, Nandita's mother's teacher, an Anglicized and skeptical man, is directed in a dream by Kali's saint, Ramakrishna, to offer his salutations at the same temple. He comes to realize that the goddess looks out for her own, here Nandita's mother, a devotee. Experiences also have a powerful sensory (therefore "real") dimension, especially involving visual "proof" where gurus, for example, are actually seen floating on water, or when they are seen to effect the long-distance psychic healing of a beloved disciple. Sumona "sees" her offering of food to Kali on the goddess herself, at her home altar, and interprets the "dark" children's disappearance and reappearance as Kali/Sakti's unpredictable ways. As such, these are experiences within a personally felt, seen, and therefore "real" connection between guru and/or deity and disciple/devotee. Where rebirth is a possibility, it is not surprising that, for example, a loving relationship with the guru can result in his birth again within a disciple's family, as in Babul's story.[1]

What is actually seen, heard, or felt by an individual disciple or devotee in a "real" event is also an ontologically "true" event, understood within the overarching conception of Sakti as a fluid, mysterious, eternal, and moral power that permeates the physical world of objects, effects, humans, and human actions. In ritual such power may infuse substances like the blood from a person's body offered to the goddess toward some desired effect, restoring an ailing child to health. It is Sakti that connects a disciple through his or her guru with the deity, Truth writ large. As the guru/deity's "compassion," Sakti is also the emotion that infuses the food that is offered to the deity, food then returned to the disciple as divine "grace," prasad, who then consumes this in an act of communion. In other contexts the guru's sakti is the willed and loving "cause" of manifestations such as white kittens, moving lights, dream-instructions, healing across distances, or the guru himself taking on the "weight" of a beloved disciple's illness. Sakti is what is *truly* real. It is the workings of this "power," where "experience" as anubhuti intimates that reality, that moves so many to deep emotion, where exegesis of a symbol or concept (Kali, Sakti), transcends its "meaning" and becomes meaningful.

The narratives of devotees' experiences suggest a unique cultural and colloquial view of the *man*, a discourse which reflects this faculty's articulation in philosophical discourse. It is the *man* which perceives that which is being communicated through experiences, as anubhuti, which reflects on, and remembers the event. It is where deity and/or guru "call" the devotee. Emotions like sorrow, fear, doubt, love, and yearning are experienced in the *man*. It has its own and "secret words," maner katha, a means whereby a worshiper speaks silently to, or supplicates divine power.

The journey of the "self," atman, in its quest for larger truths—in its transformation, both in life, but also at a cosmic level—is described by devotees as the "rites of the *man*," maner samskar. Neither the *man* nor the "memories," smrti, it records are limited to one life but to many. Smrti, in this context, makes of the ordinary, linear historicity of life-events something mythical, and transcendent of time as we know it. It is noteworthy that Kali's devotees rarely specify a date, a year, or time in their recollections. Smrti, by this definition, hints at (how can one know?) a being and actions in lives past, yielding fruits in the present, with implications for lives to come. Such accounts, then, are smaller stories, remembrances of and reflections upon wondrous "insights" constituting the larger and ongoing story of a devotee's life. The *meaningfulness* of the stories lies in this expanded context, that which is beyond the merely "real." The *man*, then, is where Sakti/sakti, as experience of divine compassion, protection, and love is most crucially and simultaneously *felt* and known. It is the "space" (but not a "place") which maybe pacified or "cooled," where final stasis from the turbulence of rebirth (and re-dying and re-suffering) is sought. Appropriately, the *man* is associated with the darkness of Kali, where all colors are absorbed and in whom, like the cool night, one seeks to find refuge and final peace in a very long journey. Kali is "received" in the *man*, this is where the journey, in this life, and for now, ends. So Bani suggests this temporary and restful halting place—is a "holiday." It is here that experiences are interpreted, where a symbol's meaning becomes meaningful.

Experiences related to the rite of sacrificial offering to the Sakti goddess, balidan, while not expressed in the language of anubhuti but in terms of "well-being," mangal, and "calamity," amangal, also point to the auspicious and to-be-hoped for forward movement in life, but also to an "obstruction," a stoppage. Balidan's deeper meaning points to a larger truth, and a transformation over many lives as the human/"self," atman, is "distilled" and "digested" in the bowels of time toward ultimate liberation. Mangal, then, is a condition sought toward well-being—in the ethical life, progeny, and material comfort—in this life, but also in lives to come. Amangal, as the consequences of an "obstructed" sacrifice, may be experienced in this life as some form of calamity including untimely death and financial ruin, but also in unknown ways in future lives, and even in future generations of the sacrifier's family. But amangal also notes the not-always-obvious flaws in the present moral character of the sacrifier—which could have accrued over previous lives. Where experiences yielding "insight," anubhuti, are generally seen as related to the moral caliber of the devotee, in the case of balidan the sacrifier is seen as responsible for the well-being or otherwise of a family, and even a lineage, here, and in the hereafter. So, in the incantation preceding the rite of sacrifice he offers himself, with true intent, and in his *man*, to the goddess.

Finally, for Kali's devotees, it is (implicitly) my own *man* that empathizes with, and respects the accounts of their experiences and how they understood these. My place in the scheme of things, in their perspective, allows that special understanding, of what their accounts truly suggest—the larger story. Their recollections, as smrti, are contingent upon a particular encounter, here with myself, possibly a devotee but also ethnographer, fulfilling, again possibly, some directive from a past life to record their perceptions of their beloved mother Kali. Their smrti remain for me to record in writing, in this book—Sakti at play again, in her infinite mystery. As with many an ethnographer, I have learned from my participants of the possible. I too have changed.

I conclude with Bani's last anubhuti, an account toward the end of her recollections. She remembered another dream she had had of Kali, as Ma Bhabatarini, who appeared to her during worship, sat to her left side, and declared that she, the goddess, is "real."

"I could not speak of this to anyone—I am opening my *man* to speak to you," Bani said to me. "But for three days my left side tingled. Can this be true? My gurudev said, 'Bani, don't speak of these anubhuti to anyone, write all these down, with their dates. One day these will be of use to you.' I said, 'No, what use can they be to me? Whoever comes to me, I'll bring them to you.' Now I think, why did I not write down those dates? He told me repeatedly . . ."

I asked her why she regretted that she had not recorded the dates. She replied:

These are smrti, after all. They are in my *man*—as I speak to you, I experience a shiver, see? I cannot make you understand, just talking to you about it. Those who haven't received these anubhuti, how can I make them understand? Those who have received even a little they will seek more. This is true. That there is a Sakti given shape as Kali on which one may call—in a crisis, even in joy. For both, our eyes fill with tears. For both we find our "holiday" in the Mother. Where does faith come from? Not from nothing. We don't always . . . connect cause and effect . . . we don't know why we suffer. . . . But [thinking of Kali] the *man* becomes quiet.

Bani appeared to suggest that her guru, with his prescient powers, possibly predicted my presence at some point in the future in her life—when an accurate historical record of her experiences, in actual time, would have been of "use" in *my* writing of them, and validated their authenticity. My presence in her life, I understood her to say, is "caused" at this juncture in time as much by my own "good works" in an earlier life as by her own spiritual accretions of merit over many lives. I too cannot know. But it is a fact, and "real" that I am an ethnographer, recording Bani's smrti, her recollections of how she came to "receive" and thus to "know" Kali.

NOTE

1. See Dr. Ian Stevenson's considerable opus on carefully documented cases of reincarnation, largely in India, notably *Unlearned Language* (1984), a project on which I assisted him. Stevenson insisted on not "explaining" his case studies, because he could not, other than within the pervasive belief in rebirth that allowed such cases to come to light.

Afterword

I followed up with some of my participants I had met in the first phase of research when I went again to Kolkata in the fall of 1992, now on a post-doctoral research grant. I also met some new people, a husband-wife couple, both academics, who were introduced to me by Alokebabu, but would hear no stories of the "miraculous" from them. Dipa's husband asked for and read my horoscope (made by an astrologer at my birth, and carefully kept by my father) and had interestingly accurate observations about my past—and fairly accurate predictions about my future (I can now look back in retrospect!). I met (now late) Sri Rabindra Mohan Roy at this time (I have referred to him in the book, in the context of his thoughts on some concepts). Bimala, who had turned atheist after her husband's sudden demise in December 1986, however, invited me to the annual celebration of Kali's festival at her maternal niece's home in southwest Kolkata. Here I would hear the story of the "alive," jagrata "Golden Kali" image on their home altar, the unusual circumstances of its provenance, and the goddess' miraculous interventions.

Sumona and her son shared more stories of her now-late husband, Sachin's, experiences. For this struggling family, I myself would bring some small joy, perhaps miraculously, to her son, a story I share later in this Afterword.

However, especially fortuitous would be my re-connecting by email with Sri Rabindra Mohan Roy's son, Amlan in 2019. I had first met Amlan in the home of a neighbor in the high rise where my father resided. An independent academic in Kolkata, he continues to correspond with me today. Amlan followed up, with enthusiasm, an "older sister's" request to let me know about Alokebabu. He did so in the current pandemic, despite my entreaties to do this by phone, going in person several times to the little temple to meet with Alokebabu's successor as priest at the little Kali temple, Kedarbabu,[1] and emailing me his "report" (November 3, 2020). Amlan informed me of

Alokebabu's passing in 2003. I briefly describe below my encounters in this second phase of work. I end with my reflections on "remembrance," smrti, in objects, acts, words, and in relationships—possibly over lifetimes—as recorded in this book.

Bimala was older and more grey, and now on her own. We sat on her neatly-made bed, in an inner and cooler room in the apartment she had shared with her late husband. She spoke of her loneliness, her struggle to sustain her spirits, of coping with her changed circumstances—and of her vulnerability as an older woman who must deal with dismissive bureaucrats when she picked up her pension at the post office. She was hesitant, when I asked, if I could talk with her about my Kali project as she was, she said, now "different." I asked how so, and she, in reply handed me a book questioning the validity of astrology, the third, she noted, in a series of works skeptical of the paranormal and "irrational" phenomena. She was now, she declared, a devotee of the book's author. Her apartment, with its bric-a-brac, mementoes of her travels, evoked memories of better days when she had enjoyed the financial stability and her husband's protection. She spoke of a son now living abroad with his wife, and far from her. I am, I reflect in my journal, a transient from America, whom she was happy to see, and to share some part of the life she now lived. We caught up with our lives, and all that had transpired over the years since we had last met.

Bimala invited me to the festivities on Kali's annual festival (October 25, 1992) at her married niece, Sumita's home. This was, unlike the event I had attended at her own mother's home in my first phase of work, a much grander event where by tradition over the years neighbors and friends had been invited to celebrate with the family. I commented on the beauty of the small eleven-inch high black stone image of Kali. Women in the family were applying *alpona*, a white rice paste, along with vermilion paste, in elaborate designs at the base of a four-foot-high altar.

Sumita's father in law, Tushar, shared the story of the Kali image. He began by commenting that the image had been found in a prostitute's home, then hesitated, uncertain about my sensibilities. I pressed him to tell me the story. His brother, he said, in his travels, had purchased a "jointed" Kali. He explained when I asked that the image's arms were screwed on and could be detached for ease of transportation. The image was even screwed on to Siva, on whom the goddess stood. He expressed some dissatisfaction with such an idea, given that a piecemeal image was antithetical to the concept of the divine as "whole."

However, he continued, on Kali's annual festival in 1952 or 1953, as friends and relatives arrived at their home and were waiting for worship to begin, the "jointed" Kali fell from his brother's hands and broke into pieces: "How ashamed my brother felt! It was a matter of his honor!" His brother, weeping, feared that "calamity." amangal, would befall him and that his patri-line would come to an end. Tushar, who loved his brother dearly, wondered what he himself could do about this situation. He went "immediately" with his brother and a friend to Kalighat (the area surrounding the Temple), and asked the touts (who assist with pilgrims visiting Kalighat Temple) if they could help him purchase an image of the goddess. The touts suggested that at this last minute the best option was to purchase a clay image readily avail-able for purchase from the many shops in the area. Finally, a tout who had seen a Kali image in a prostitute's room took them to the extensive brothels in the vicinity of Kalighat Temple. The brothers waited: "We were ready to pay anything," said Tushar. The tout brought out the image, the brothers paid him and took it home.

The stone image was washed with soap, ritually bathed with appropriate chants, and then also ritually invested with life. Unlike images of deities at the conclusion of annual festivals, which are ritually bade farewell and cast into running waters, this Kali, I was told, would be housed permanently at Tushar's home, worshiped daily, and never bade farewell. The image was decorated with real gold ornaments (a tiara, necklace, bracelets and girdle) in the early years of its worship (hence its name, the "golden" Kali). Bimala, at some point and evidently a believer at the time, had gifted a gold tongue, eyes, brows, and teeth to be affixed on the image. However, her family described at least two attempts by thieves to steal the gold, but each time the ornaments were recovered. In one account a thief suddenly terrified at what he had done, became confused and was apprehended by neighbors. His fears were attributed by the family to their "alive" Kali. The image was kept in a specially built room on the rooftop of the house and behind an iron grill which would be locked at night. On Kalipuja the grill was pushed back (as I saw) and the image, now adorned, was displayed for worship. After Tushar's father died the family wanted to stop the annual celebration, but the commu-nity would not allow it. So, some forty years after the Golden Kali had arrived at this house, the goddess' worship continued.

Sumona recognized me immediately as I approached their door, and, call-ing me by name, invited me in. She said she was full of joy (ananda) that their "daughter" had remembered them. The room looked much the same as it had before. At first I did not notice the photograph of Sachin hanging above the bed on the wall, garlanded with Siva's garland of wooden beads. But then I did. What I had feared had indeed happened—Sachin had died a year before, almost to the day. I told mother and son how grieved I was to hear this news. Sumona told me how delighted Sachin had been to receive a letter from me, from the United States, and that he had kept the letter carefully in his copy of the *Mahabharata*. In response, he had enclosed a flower from his worship in an envelope, and asked his brother to mail it to me from the main post office in central Kolkata to ensure that it would reach me. It did not, I said to Sumona. I had brought the acknowledgments page from my dissertation to give to them. Mukul would frame it, she said, in "remembrance," smrti, both as a gift from me for his father, and in remembrance of his father.

Mukul, now twenty-four, told me about his father's last illness and final days at a Kolkata hospital. Sachin had developed a viral fever, then suffered a stroke, and also what sounded to me like pneumonia. Sadly, his passing had left his family even more destitute than before. Sachin's tea firm had bilked him out of a large sum of money that was owed to him. Sachin had also invested Rupees 25,000 (around $400) in a savings and loan company which had gone under. Sumona was the same (though older) thin, suffering person I had met last in 1987. At this meeting too I would hear more stories about Sachin's powers. Sachin had, she said, been her husband of many years (as her eyes filled with tears). But her son was there. She quietly peeled the leaves of the wood apple (bel) tree, sacred to Siva, as she wove a garland of red hibiscus for worship. She had been in a state of ritual pollution since Sachin's death a year ago, and had not visited Kalighat Temple, but had worshiped at home. Mukul picked up the story of his father's continuing presence in their lives:

> My father still comes to me in my dreams. He loved me so much, and he calls me. He used to predict my exam grades—in detail! He used to warn me sometimes of danger. He was often right, and I have often escaped being hurt or even being killed in such situations. I used to work in the youth wing of the Congress party, and [rival] Communist youth cadres would try to beat me up.

But Mukul now had a job as a salesman with a roofing company, earning around $160 a month, which he said, has kept them from starving. But his dreams and ambitions were on hold:

> I haven't been able to go to college as I wanted to. How could I, with the hours I work? Still, I'm doing it for the sake of a better life for my mother, though I wasn't able to do much for my father. I've been working ever since I was in Class 8.

And then our story, his, mine and Sachin's took an interesting turn, as he said:

"I would love to own a motorbike. Young men my age love speed—but how can I afford it? I really like American jeans. Could you send me a pair?"

I told him that, given the vagaries of the Indian postal service, such a parcel might never arrive at his door. However, I said, it so happened that I had brought a pair for a nephew, and that they had been too small for him. I said to Mukul: "It's a coincidence, but I have a pair with me which a friend is presently trying to sell off. If she still has them you can try them on. If they fit you, they're yours."

Two days after we met, Mukul came to visit me at my father's apartment to try on the Levis that I had retrieved from my friend. They fit him and I gave them to him. He asked if he should pay me. I refused his offer, as my father commented, "Take the jeans. Your older sister is giving them to you." He was delighted with his gift, and I was happy that I could give him something he had so wanted. I reflected that perhaps this small incident could be seen as the working out of events and relationships that transcended time as we knew it. When I first met Mukul and his mother years before, Sumona had repeatedly told me how close her son and husband were, how Sachin had loved his son "blindly." Perhaps a loving father now watched over his beloved son as I, an "agent," yatri, of divine will—in that mysterious "play" of Sakti—could give this young man the jeans he had so desired and could not afford to buy. Did a father's sakti, through me, fulfill a beloved son's wish?

Debu, the caretaker at Kalighat Temple, had forgotten my name, though he recognized me. I gave his wife a bottle of cologne I had brought with me, as a gift. She said she would first offer it to the goddess on the auspicious eighth day of worship for the goddess Durga, coming up shortly. Debu commented on the deity-devotee relationship, and that his wife would use nothing until it had been offered to her Mother. Debu, like Sumona, observed that even as people go away, a connection, once forged, is not lost, it remains as smrti. He invited me to photograph the elaborate ritual offerings on Osthomi, and the ritual offering of food, bhog, to the goddess ten days later at the Temple. After the worship on Osthomi, which I did photograph, Debu, putting vermilion on the women present, blessed me with his hope that I have an "auspicious" future: "All that your *man* desires may these be fulfilled." I have held those words close to my heart over these many years.

I first met Sri Rabindra Mohan Roy, Amlan's father, at his home in late September, then twice again after that. He "knew" by looking at me, he said at that first meeting, referring to his knowledge of astrology, that he and I were "compatible," called me "daughter," and said he would speak with me. He established at the start my place in the larger scheme of things. He observed that Western concepts of free will and Hindu concepts of reincarnation are illustrated in the story of a cow tethered to a stake. The animal doesn't know that there is a rope around its neck if it does not stray too far. It thinks it is free, but it is not. This is an illusion. In this context, Roy noted that he and I have a long connection, where merit accumulated over lifetimes is at work. I had been impelled, thus, towards my research as a consequence of lifetimes of accumulated merit, he said, and that our meeting had been predicted for this time and place. My choice of research topic had not, by this reasoning, been a free one!

Roy discoursed on the question first posed rhetorically by Alokebabu, "Who am 'I'"? The East, he noted, recognized that this 'I' can only be subjectively "experienced"—he used the word 'anubhav'—and not through objective analysis which was a style of discourse he attributed to the West. Even as his wife, Amlan's mother, served me delicious sweets he gave me an impromptu initiation, diksa, suggesting I remember the 'seed incantation' he chose to give me, in times of crisis. I reflect in my journal: "It's interesting that he should give me this particular mantra [which I may not reveal]. . . . Somewhere my research into the nature of religious experience and the deity-devotee relationship—where am I, the researcher, in all this? Indeed, who *am* 'I'?" (I don't of course have an answer as of this writing).

In 2020, Amlan informed me that Alokebabu had passed away on June 5, 2003.[2] Kedarbabu was now the priest of the little temple, and Amlan met him on his third attempt. This priest had been designated formally by Alokebabu to now operate the temple. Sixty-two years old, Amlan describes Kedarbabu as "intelligent-looking, bright-eyed," with thinning hair but not bald. Kedarbabu's face, Amlan continues, "fascinated" him. Slightly built, of medium height, with a "sparse beard and a manner of grave courtesy behind which lay considerable firmness of character," the priest is "distinguished looking, with soothing eyes and a lofty forehead," dark-skinned, with a "placid countenance showing deep spiritual engagement, which he learned from [his preceptor, Alokebabu]."

Amlan spends a few hours with the priest, whom he describes as Alokebabu's "spiritual heir." Kedarbabu talks briefly about his own family: a wife, and a son who works in insurance, but mostly about his preceptor. Alokebabu, the priest says, called his disciples to him shortly before his death for final instructions, and handed over responsibilities for worship and temple maintenance to him, Kedarbabu, who was "closest" to him. He then said he would not be talk further with anyone (in keeping with the often-brusque man of few words I knew).

Kedarbabu described Alokebabu as a "realized" or "enlightened man" (*siddha purusa*), a man he respected highly. He himself was not "schooled," and had come as an adolescent to the Kali temple to assist Alokebabu, who would be his mentor. Uneducated in Sanskrit, Kedarbabu had learned the rules of worship from his mentor. The older man would evidently find in this unschooled youth some spiritual potential—something Kedarbabu could not have foretold, given more educated persons who came to see Alokebabu. However, Alokebabu had had "inner" knowledge of him, and had laid the "spiritual foundation" for his disciple.

This is a book about more than, I think, those who were "participants" in my research project on "Kali in Bengali lives." It is about relationships, some who saw me as a daughter (like Sumona), those I called "aunt" (like Bimala), others who served as instructors and mentors to one who sought to learn (Debu, Alokebabu, Sri Rabindra Mohan Roy), and those who saw me as an older sister (Didi), like Amlan and Mukul. Words, acts, and objects invested those relationships with meaning, beyond the kin terms themselves. A wonderful, personally cooked meal shared, lively conversations with Bimala; afternoons spent at Alokebabu's temple, as he spoke about his Mother Kali, denying "magic" until he did not, at the end; Sumona's warm welcome, no matter her life of hardship and penury, her own stories of the goddess' compassion, but also about her husband, Sachin's experiences; not least the Levis I could gift to their son, Mukul—memories which are for me evocative, happy, and warm, sustained even after decades.

Remembrance, as smrti, as I understand this, constitutes all this and more. It is a page from my dissertation given to Sachin's son, saying I remember his father, with respect and gratitude for sharing his stories. It is Debu's words of blessing for me, wishing me mangal, an auspicious future, and that my *man*'s desires be fulfilled; it is Sri Rabindra Mohan Roy's words, echoed in those of others, that even as we make these memories today, smrti connects us over our many lives, transcending time and space, giving meaning and context to our meeting today, in this place and at this time. So Bani says, she should have written and kept records of her experiences, for me to write her story, in her remembrance, and in my writing of her experiences, as smrti. However, even without formal "records" I have written her story in this book.

In my last meeting with Alokebabu in November 1992, as I prepared to return to the United States, I gave him books on teaching the Bengali alphabet, other books of rhymes for children, and wax crayons, for his free school—but no money. In this final meeting Alokebabu commented that he had respected my steadfast efforts. He then gave me, from his worship and as "grace," prasad, leaves from the wood apple tree, sacred to Siva and smeared with sandalwood paste. I have kept this object over these many years, in an envelope clipped to my journal, as smrti, of a spiritually powerful man without whom this work might not have found fruition.

NOTES

1. I have changed this priest's name.
2. Amlan called this an "assignment" given him by his "older sister," myself. The words in quotation marks are from his email.

Appendix

Select Names of Deities, Concepts, and Texts, with Diacritical Marks

DEITIES

Ātman
Bhagavān
Dakṣiṇā Kālī
Durgā
Gaṇeśa
Hanumān
Jāgrata
Kṛṣṇa
Lakṣmī
Prakṛti
Śakti
Śākta
Śiva
Tārā
Viṣṇu/Vaiṣṇava

CONCEPTS AND OBJECTS USED IN WORSHIP

Anubhūti
āratī
darśan
dīkṣā
dṛṣṭi
hōma
iṣṭadevī

kṛpā
līlā
māyā
mōkṣa
prasād
pūjā
samsāra
smṛti
sukṛti
svapnādeś

TEXTS

Devī-Mahātmya
Kathāmṛta
Mārkendeya Purāṇa
Rudhīrādhyāya
Śrī Śrī Gurugītā
Śrī Śrī Kālīpūjā Paddhati
Tantrasār
Upaniṣad
Vedānta

Bibliography

Abrahams, Roger D. "Ordinary and Extraordinary Experience." In *The Anthropology of Experience*, edited by Victor Turner and Edward M. Bruner, 45–72. Urbana, IL: University of Illinois Press, 1986.

Appadurai, Arjun, Frank J. Korom, and Margaret A. Mills, eds. *Gender, Genre, and Power in South Asian Expressive Traditions*. Philadelphia, PA: University of Pennsylvania Press, 1991.

Atmarupananda, Swami. "Cultural Presuppositions as Determinants in Experience: A Comparison of Some Basic Indian and Western Concepts." In *Concepts of Knowledge: East and West. Papers from a Seminar*, 4–10 January, 1995. Kolkata: The Ramakrishna Mission Institute of Culture, 2000: 20–43.

Avalon, Sir Arthur. *Sakti and Sakta*. New York: Dover Publications, Inc., 1978.

Babb, Lawrence A. "The Food of the Gods in Chattisgarh: Some Structural Features of Hindu Ritual." *Southwestern Journal of Anthropology* 26, no. 3 (1970): 287–304.

———. "Glancing: Visual Interaction in Hinduism." *Journal of Anthropological Research* 37, no. 4 (1981): 387–401.

———. *Redemptive Encounters: Three Modern Styles in the Hindu Tradition*. Berkeley, CA: University of California Press, 1986.

Basu Roy, Indrani. *Kalighat, its Impact on Socio-cultural Life of Hindus*. New Delhi: Gyan Publishing House, 1993.

Bhattacharya, Pandit Srimohan. "The Use of the Word Prama: Valid Cognition in Advaita Vedanta." *Concepts of Knowledge. East and West. Papers from a Seminar*, 4–10 January, 1995. 2000: 83–92.

Blaquiere, W. C. Esq., Trans. "The *Rudhiradhyaya*." In *Asiatic Researches*, vol. 5, 371–391. New Delhi: Cosmo Publications, 1979.

Bruner, Jerome . "Life as Narrative." *Social Research* 54, no. 1 (1987): 11–32.

Budhananda, Swami. *The Mind and its Control*. Calcutta, West Bengal: Advaita Ashrama, 1991.

Caldwell, Sarah. "Margins at the Center: Tracing Kali Through Time, Space, and Culture." In *Encountering Kali: In the Margins, at the Center, in the West*, edited by Rachel McDermott and Jeffrey J. Kripal, 249–272. Berkeley, CA: University of California Press, 2005.

Coburn, Thomas B. *Devi-Mahatmya: The Crystallization of the Goddess Tradition.* Delhi, India: Motilal Banarsidass, 1984.

Copeman, Jacob, and Aya Ikegame, eds. *The Guru in South Asia: New Interdisciplinary Perspectives.* London and New York: Routledge, South Asian Studies Series, 2012.

Crites, Stephen. "The Narrative Quality of Experience." *Journal of the American Academy of Religion* 39, no. 1 (1971): 291–311.

Das, Veena. "Language of Sacrifice." *MAN* n.s. 18, no. 3 (1983): 445–462.

Dasgupta, R. K. "Foreword: Swami Vivekananda's Concept of Knowledge." In *Concepts of Knowledge: East and West*, vii–viii, 1995.

Dempsey, Corinne G., and Selva J. Raj, eds. *Miracle as Modern Conundrum in South Asian Religious Traditions.* Albany, NY: SUNY Press, 2008.

Dev, A. T. *Dev's Concise Dictionary: Bengali to English. An Up-to-Date Dictionary Containing Current Words & Phrases.* Calcutta: B.C. Majumdar, Dev Press, 1985.

Eck, Diane L. *Darshan: Seeing the Divine Image in India.* Chambersburg, PA: Anima Publications, 1981.

———. *Encountering God: A Spiritual Journey from Bozeman to Banaras.* Boston, MA: Beacon Press, 2003.

Embree, Ainslie T. *The Hindu Tradition: Readings in Oriental Thought.* New York, NY: Vintage Books, 1972.

Foulston, Lynn, and Stuart Abbott. *Hindu Goddesses: Beliefs and Practices.* Brighton and Portland: Sussex University Press, 2009.

Gatwood, Lynn E. *Devi and the Spouse Goddess: Women, Sexuality and Marriages in India.* Riverdale, MD: The Riverdale Co., 1985.

Geertz, Clifford. "Making Experience, Authoring Selves." In *The Anthropology of Experience*, edited by Victor Turner and Edward M. Bruner, 373–380. Urbana, IL: University of Illinois Press, 1986.

Gold, Ann Grodzins. "Showing Miracles in Rajasthan: Proof and Grace," In *The Miracle as Modern Conundrum in South Asian Religious Traditions*, edited by Selva Raj and Corinne Dempsey. Albany, NY: State University of New York, 2008: 85–104.

Gold, Daniel. "Continuities as Guru's Change." In *The Guru in South Asia: New Interdisciplinary Perspectives*, edited by Jacob Copeman and Aya Ikegame, 241–254. New York and London: Routledge, 2012.

Goonasekera, Sunil. "Kataragama and the Tsunami." In Raj and Dempsey, op. cit., 2008: 57–81.

Harman, William P. "A Miracle (or Two) in Tiruchirapalli." In Raj and Dempsey, op. cit., 2008: 105–118.

Hawley, John Stratton. *A Storm of Songs.* Cambridge, MA: Harvard University Press, 2015.

Hayley, Audrey. "A Commensal Relationship with God: The Nature of the Offering in Assamese Vaishnavism." In *Sacrifice*, edited by Michael F. C. Bourdillon and Meyer Fortes, 107–125. New York: Academic Press, Inc., 1980.

Hiltebeitel, Alf, and Katherine M. Erndl, eds. *Is the Goddess a Feminist? The Politics of South Asian Goddesses.* New York: New York University Press, 2000.

Hubert, H., and M. Mauss. *Sacrifice: Its Nature and Function.* Translated by W. D. Halls. Chicago, IL: University of Chicago Press, 1964.

Inden, Ronald B., and Ralph W. Nicholas. *Kinship in Bengali Culture.* Chicago, IL: University of Chicago Press, 1977.

Johnson, Mark. "The Imaginative Basis of Meaning and Cognition." In *Images of Memory: On Remembering and Representation*, edited by Suzanne Kuchler and Walter S. Melion, 74–86. Washington and London: Smithsonian Institution Press, 1991.

Kakar, Sudhir. *Shamans, Mystics and Doctors*. Chicago, IL: University of Chicago Press, 1982.

Kaviraj, Gopinath. *Tantra o Agamsastrer Digdarshan*. Calcutta Sanskrit College Research Series No. XXV. Calcutta: Sanskrit College, 1963.

Khare, Ravindra. *The Hindu Hearth and Home*. New Delhi: Vikas Publishing House Pvt. Ltd., 1976.

———. "Presentations and Prayers: Two Homologous Systems in Northern India." In *The New Wind: Changing Identities in South Asia*, edited by K. David, 105–131. The Hague & Paris: Mouton Press, 1977.

Kinsley, David R. *The Sword and the Flute: Kali and Krishna: Dark Visions of the Terrible and Sublime in Hindu Mythology*. Berkeley, CA: University of California Press, 1975a.

———. "Freedom from Death in the Worship of Kali." *Numen* 22, no. 3 (1975b): 183–207.

———. "Blood and Death Out of Place: Reflections on the Goddess Kali." In *The Divine Consort: Radha and the Goddesses of India*, edited by John Stratton Hawley and Donna Marie Wulff, 144–152. Berkeley, CA: Berkeley Religious Studies Series, 1982.

———. *The Hindu Goddess: Visions of the Divine Feminine in the Hindu Religious Tradition*. Berkeley, CA: University of California Press, 1986.

———. *The Goddess' Mirror: Visions of the Divine from East to West*. Albany: SUNY Press, 1989.

———. "Kali. Blood and Death Out of Place." In *Devi: Goddesses of India*, edited by John Stratton Hawley and Donna Marie Wulff, 77–86. Berkeley and Los Angeles: University of California Press, 1996.

Kripal, Jeffrey J. "Perfecting the Mother's Silence: Dream, Devotion, and Family in the Deification of Sharada Devi." In *Seeking Mahadevi: Constructing the Identities of the Hindu Great Goddess*, edited by Tracy Pintchman, 171–197. Albany, NY: SUNY Press, 2001.

———. *Authors of the Impossible: The Paranormal and the Sacred*. Chicago, IL: University of Chicago Press, 2010.

Kuchler, Suzanne, and Walter S. Melion, eds. *Images of Memory: On Remembering and Representation*. Washington, D.C.: Smithsonian Institution Press, 1991.

Mackenzie-Brown, C. "Kali the Mad Mother." In *The Book of the Goddess: Past and Present*, edited by C. Olson, 110–123. New York, NY: The Crossroad Publishing Co., 1985.

Matilal, Bimal K. *The Logical Illumination of Indian Mysticism*. Oxford: Clarendon Press, 1977.

———. *Logic, Language & Reality: An Introduction to Indian Philosophical Studies*. Delhi: Motilal Banarsidass, 1985.

———. *Perception: An Essay on Classical Indian Theories of Knowledge*. Oxford: Clarendon Press, 1986.

McDaniel, June. *The Madness of the Saints: Ecstatic Religion in Bengal*. Chicago, IL: University of Chicago Press, 1989.

McDermott, Rachel Fell. "Epilogue: The Western Kali." In *Devi: Goddesses of India*, edited by John Stratton Hawley and Donna Marie Wolff. Berkeley, CA: University of California Press, 1996: 281–313.

———. "A Festival for Jagaddhatri and the Power of Localized Religion in West Bengal," In *Breaking Boundaries with the Goddess. New Directions in the Study of Saktism*, edited by Cynthia Ann Humes and Rachel Fell McDermott. *Essays in honor of Narendranath Bhattacharya*. New Delhi: Manohar Publishing, 2009: 201–221.

———. *Mother of My Heart, Daughter of My Dreams: Kali and Uma in the Devotional Poetry of Bengal*. Oxford: Oxford University Press, 2001.

———. "Kali's New Frontiers: A Hindu Goddess on the Internet." In *Encountering Kali: In the Margins, at the Center, in the West*, edited by Rachel Fell McDermott and Jeffrey J. Kripal, 273–295. Berkeley, CA: University of California Press, 2003.

McDermott, Rachel Fell, and Jeffrey J. Kripal, eds. *Encountering Kali: In the Margins, at the Center, in the West*. Berkeley, CA: University of California Press, 2003.

Mlecko, Joel D. "The Guru in the Hindu Tradition." *Numen* 29, no. 1 (1982): 33–61.

Monier-Williams, M. "Indian Wisdom." *The Chowkhamba Sanskrit Studies* XXXVI (1963).

———. *Sanskrit-English Dictionary*. Oxford: Clarendon Press, 1964.

Moodie, Deonnie. *The Making of a Modern Temple and a Hindu City: Kalighat and Kolkata*. Oxford: Oxford University Press, 2018.

Mookerjee, A., and M. Khanna. *The Tantric Way*. Boston: New York Graphic Society, 1977.

Murray, Michael. "Narrative Data." In *The SAGE Handbook of Qualitative Data Collection*. SAGE Publications Ltd, edited by Uwe Flick. Thousand Oaks, CA and London, U.K.: SAGE Publications Ltd. 2018: 264–286. [http://dx.doi.org/10.4135/9781526416070.n17].

Narayan, Kirin. *Storytellers, Saints, and Scoundrels*. Philadelphia: University of Pennsylvania Press, 1989.

Neumann, Erich. *The Great Mother: An Analysis of the Archetype*. Translated by Ralph Mannheim. Bollingen Series, volume 47, 2nd ed. New York: Pantheon Books, 1963.

Obeyesekere, Gananath. *The Awakened Ones: Phenomenology of Visionary Experience*. New York, NY: Columbia University Press, 2012.

Parry, Jonathan. "Death and Digestion: The Symbolism of Food and Eating in North Indian Mortuary Rites." *MAN* n.s. 20, no. 4 (1985): 612–629.

Pechilis, Karen. *Interpreting Devotion: The Poetry and Legacy of a Female Bhakti Saint of India*. London and New York: Routledge, 2012.

Potter, K. H., ed. *Encyclopedia of Indian Philosophies: Indian Metaphysics and Epistemology: The Tradition of Nyaya-Vaisesika up to Gangesa*. Princeton, NJ: Princeton University Press, 1977.

Presti, David, ed. *Mind beyond Brain, Buddhism, Science, and the Paranormal*. New York: Columbia University Press, 2018.

Raj, Selva J. "An Ethnographic Encounter with the Wondrous in a South Indian Catholic Shrine." In *The Miracle as Modern Conundrum in South Asian Religious Traditions*, edited by Selva J. Raj and Corinne G. Dempsey, 141–166. Albany, NY: State University of New York, 2008.

Raj, Selva J., and Corinne G. Dempsey, eds. *The Miracle as Modern Conundrum in South Asian Religious Traditions*. Albany, NY: State University of New York, 2008.

Rawson, P. *Tantra: The Indian Cult of Ecstasy*. New York, NY: Avon Books, 1973.

Ray, A. K. "A Short History of Calcutta: Town and Suburbs." In *Census*, volume VII, 1901, Pt. 1. Calcutta, West Bengal: Rddhi-India, 1982.

Ray, Alok, ed. *Calcutta Keepsake*. Calcutta, West Bengal: Rddhi-India, 1980.

Ray, N. R., ed. *H.E.A. Cotton's "Calcutta Old and New."* Calcutta, West Bengal: S.C. Das, 1980.

Revathi, S. "Consciousness: Its Relation to Mind According to Advaita." In *Life, Mind, Consciousness: Papers Read at an International Seminar Held at the Ramakrishna Mission Institute of Culture*, 335–354, Kolkata, January 16–18. Kolkata: RKMIC, 2004.

Rinehart, Robin. "The Neo-Vedanta Miracle." In Raj and Dempsey, eds., op. cit., 2008: 23–38.

Samanta, Suchitra. "Recollection and Cognition: A Bengali Devotee Remembers How She "Received" the Goddess Kali." *Unpublished Paper Presented at the Symposium on Myth, Memory, and History*, University of Virginia, Charlottesville, VA, Spring, 1992a.

———. "*Mangalmayima, Sumangali, Mangal*: Bengali Perceptions of the Divine Feminine, Motherhood, and 'Auspiciousness'." *Contributions to Indian Sociology* 26, no. 1 (1992b): 51–75.

———. "The 'Self-Animal' and Divine Digestion: Goat Sacrifice to the Goddess Kali in Bengal." *Journal of Asian Studies* 53, no. 3 (1994): 779–803.

———. "The Powers of the Guru: Sakti, "Mind," and Miracles in Narratives of Bengali Religious Experience." *Anthropology and Humanism* 23, no. 1 (1998): 30–50.

Sharadanada, Swami. *Sri RamaKrishna, the Great Master*. Madras, Tamil Nadu: Ramakrishna Math of Mylapore, 1956.

Sinha, Jadunath. *Rama Prasada's Devotional Songs: The Cult of Sakti*. Calcutta: Sinha Publishing House, 1966.

———. *Indian Epistemology of Perception*. Calcutta, West Bengal: Sinha Publishing House Pvt. Ltd., 1969.

Smith, Barbara Herrnstein. "Narrative Versions, Narrative Theories." In *On Narrative*, edited by W. J. T. Mitchell, 209–232. Chicago, IL: University of Chicago Press, 1981.

Stevenson, Ian. *Unlearned Language: New Studies in Xenoglossy*. Charlottesville, VA: University of Virginia Press, 1984.

Stromberg, Peter. *Symbols of Community: The Cultural System of a Swedish Church*. Tucson, AZ: University of Arizona Press, 1986.

Toomey, P. M. "Food from the Mouth of Krishna: Socio-Religious Aspects of Sacred Food in Two Krishnaite Sects." In *Food, Society and Culture. Aspects in South Asian Food Systems*, edited by Ravindra S. Khare and M. S. A. Rao, 55–83. Durham, NC: Carolina Academic Press, 1986.

Turner, Victor. "Dewey, Dilthey, and Drama: An Essay in the Anthropology of Experience." In *The Anthropology of Experience*, edited by Victor W. Turner and Edward M. Bruner, 33–44. Urbana, IL: University of Illinois Press, 1986.

Vail, Lisa. "Founders, Swamis, and Devotees: Becoming Divine in North Karnataka." In *Gods of Flesh, Gods of Stone: The Embodiment of Divinity in India*, edited

by J. P. Waghorne and V. Narayanan, 123–140. Chambersburg, PA: Anima
   Publications, 1985.

Wadley, Susan S., and Bruce W. Derr. "Eating Sins in Karimpur." In *India Through
   Hindu Categories*, edited by McKim Marriott, 131–148. New Delhi and Newbury
   Park, London: SAGE Publications, 1990.

Ward, Rev. William. *A View of the History, Literature and Mythology of the Hindoos*.
   London: Kingsbury, Parbury & Allen, 1822.

Warnock, Mary. *Memory*. London & Boston: Faber and Faber, 1987.

Weber, Max. *The Sociology of Religion*. Translated by Ephraim Fischoff. Boston:
   Beacon Press, 1922.

Zimmer, Heinrich. *The Art of Indian Asia: Its Mythology and Transformations*.
   Completed and edited by Joseph Campbell, volume 1. Bollingen Series, volume
   39. New York: Pantheon Books, 1955.

BENGALI SOURCES

Brahmananda, Swami. "Guru." In *Gurutattva O Gurugita*, edited by Swami
   Raghubarananda, 23–38. Calcutta, West Bengal: Udbodhan Karyalaya, 1987.

Jagadiswarananda, Swami, Trans. *Devi Mahatmya*. Calcutta, West Bengal: Udbodhan
   Karyalaya, 1985.

Nirmmalananda, Swami. *Bharate Saktipuja*. Calcutta, West Bengal: Udbodhan
   Karyalaya, 1979.

Pandit Shyamacaran Kabiratna. *SrisriKalipuja Paddhati*. Calcutta: Radha Pustakalaya,
   1981.

Raghubarananda, Swami, ed. *Gurutattva O Gurugita*. Calcutta, West Bengal:
   Udbodhan Karyalaya, 1987.

Roy, Diptimoy. *Pascimbanger Kali o Kalikshetra*. Calcutta, West Bengal: Mondol
   Book House, 1986.

Roy, N., and A. Upadhyaya. *Prachin Kalikata*. Calcutta, West Bengal: Sahityaloka,
   1983.

Sri Jatadhari Bidyaratna. *SrisriKalipuja Paddhati*. Calcutta: Sulabh Kalikata Library,
   1985.

Vivekananda, Swami. *Dhyan O Maner Sakti*. Calcutta, West Bengal: Udbodhan
   Karyalaya, 1992.

Index

About the Author

Suchitra Samanta has a BA in English literature from Kolkata University, India, Master's degree in drama (1984), and doctoral degree in cultural anthropology, both from the University of Virginia in the United States (1990). Her dissertation and earlier publications, based on field research, are on cultural aspects of religious experience and practices among devotees of the Hindu goddess Kali in Kolkata, India. Her later research and publications address Muslim women and issues of minority status, gender, poverty, and female literacy in India (2001, 2004, 2009, 2016, and 2017). Her most recent published work is on Asian American female students at community college in the United States (2018). A journal article on higher educational aspirations of recently relocated South Asian Bhutanese-Nepali refugees to the United States has been presented at several conferences, and is in progress.

Samanta's anthology, *Hauntings: Thirteen Tales by Bangla's Master Storytellers* (New Delhi: Katha, 2000, 2010) is a collection of short fiction by eminent authors in Bengali literature, selected, translated and edited by her, and highlights female protagonists.

Samanta teaches courses in the women's and gender studies program at Virginia Tech's Department of Sociology, on feminist activism, global and transnational gender inequity issues, feminist theory, and on the Asian American experience. She has received the Department of Sociology's Snizek teaching award in 2017, and the university's highest teaching award for teaching introductory courses, the Sporn award, in 2012.

www.ingramcontent.com/pod-product-compliance
Lightning Source LLC
Chambersburg PA
CBHW050612280326
41932CB00016B/3008